I Quit.

totally relate to. This is a story of strength, hope, empowerment, humor as a coping mechanism and God giving you exactly what you need when you need it.

— **Jennifer Lane**, cancerbomb.com

"Kristina Kotlus writes about her struggle with brain cancer and her very real chance of dying from it in a humorous, poignant, serious, hopeful, eye-opening, compassionate, engaging manner. She is bluntly honest about her hopes and fears, her concerns about her children, and the little kindnesses that made big differences in her recovery. She provides the reader with extremely wise and incredibly practical ways to interact with those who are dealing with cancer. She recounts instances of well-meant but thoughtless cruelty, and she praises the friends who through their love and wisdom made her struggles winnable. More importantly, she provides the story not only of how she beat cancer, but why—and sometimes the why is the most important part. As I read her book, I laughed and cried with her. If you have cancer—or any other life-threatening disease—or if you have a friend or family member who is dealing with such a diagnosis, you will want to devour this book."

— **Steve Troxel, Ph.D.**, Retired Professor, Liberty University

"In a world where most people young and old do not want to reveal what is really happening in their lives, Kristina Kotlus in her book is authentic, wearing no mask but is willing to take us with her on her journey. There are moments of emotional, physical and spiritual pain but there are also moments that reveal how she experienced those special moments when God showed up and she is filled with hope. We are all filled with fear when we are faced with challenges but as this book reveals, challenges can also transform us and in doing so others are transformed."

— **Reverend Liz Danielsen**, Chaplain-Founder/Executive Director, Spiritual Care Support Ministries, scsm.tv

"A mutual friend introduced me to Kristina Kotlus with the words, 'You two need to know each other.' As I took Kristina's outstretched hand and returned her warm smile, her first words stunned me: "I'm a brain cancer survivor; actually, I've had cancer twice." *I Quit* vividly describes the battle that tried to take her life. I'm an English teacher; I teach advanced college-level writing to juniors and seniors at a nearby university, and words are my life. That afternoon I set aside the mountain of essays I needed to grade to begin reading Kristina's words. Her story quickly engulfed me with its beautiful, poignant prose, laced with the somber reality of life and death, love and family, faith and friends—and lots of sarcasm, perfectly timed. As a lover of words, I was enchanted by her writing, and I read voraciously throughout the night. I laughed out loud in some parts, cried in others, and held my breath many times, but I could not put the book down. Kristina has written a profoundly courageous and heartwarming story, and I am honored to endorse her work. Everyone should read her book and pass it on to others. All will be richer for it."

— **Peggy Scolaro,** English Instructor,
George Mason University, Editor, *The Dream King*

I Quit.

*Facing Cancer with
Faith, Family and Friends*
(And Sarcasm. There's a lot of that, too.)

Kristina Schnack Kotlus

NASHVILLE

NEW YORK • LONDON • MELBOURNE • VANCOUVER

I Quit.

Facing Cancer with Faith, Family and Friends
(And Sarcasm. There's a lot of that, too.)

Published in New York, New York, by Morgan James Publishing. Morgan James is a trademark of Morgan James, LLC. www.MorganJamesPublishing.com

THE HOLY BIBLE, NEW INTERNATIONAL VERSION®, NIV® Copyright © 1973, 1978, 1984, 2011 by Biblica, Inc.® Used by permission. All rights reserved worldwide.

Scripture taken from the New King James Version®. Copyright © 1982 by Thomas Nelson. Used by permission. All rights reserved.

Taken from: THE PRAYER THAT CHANGES EVERYTHING® Copyright © 2004 by Stormie Omartian. Published by Harvest House Publishers, Eugene, Oregon 97408, www.harvesthousepublishers.com

ISBN 978-1-64279-531-8 paperback
ISBN 978-1-64279-532-5 eBook
Library of Congress Control Number: 2019937078

Photo Credit:
Lisa Julia Photography, http://www.lisajuliaphotography.com

Hair Credit:
Jennifer Etherington, Statements the Salon

Cover Design by:
Rachel Lopez
www.r2cdesign.com

Interior Design by:
Bonnie Bushman
The Whole Caboodle Graphic Design

In an effort to support local communities, raise awareness and funds, Morgan James Publishing donates a percentage of all book sales for the life of each book to Habitat for Humanity Peninsula and Greater Williamsburg.

Get involved today! Visit
www.MorganJamesBuilds.com

For Austin.
I couldn't ask for a bigger blessing than having you as a husband.
But if I have to get cancer one more time for you to
believe in Jesus, we're going to be in a serious fight. For real.

Table of Contents

Acknowledgements

As this is a faith book, I know that first and foremost I am supposed to thank God, and I do. In fact, this whole book is a thank you to Him. However, I also want to thank all the people whose names I did not include in that thank you. The closer I get to publishing the more I worry that I will deeply offend someone for not including their contribution to my story. I'm sorry if I didn't write your name specifically. I had a word limit. I still love you very much.

I would next like to thank my amazingly supportive family and friends. I specifically want to thank my amazing husband, Austin, for believing in my vision for this project, my mother, Lydia, for listening to me complain, my children, Riley, Logan, and Savannah for cheering me on and for showing me that my testimony can have an impact. Thank you to Kristina Nohe for being the friend willing to take a red pen to my draft, to Reverend Liz Danielsen for making sure I didn't write the next great heresy of the church, and to Chris Jones of Chris Jones, Ink for being not only an editor, but an encourager and sounding board for all my doubts.

Thank you to the amazing pastors at Chapel Springs Church who challenge me to continue to grow in my walk with Jesus, and who make me want to earn my missionary shoes. Thank you to the Soul Purpose class at Chapel Springs, which has prayed without ceasing for my healing, cheered me on with every good report, and loved me in spite of myself. Your faith makes me want to be a better Christian and I love you all so much. To all of my prayer warriors and "safe space" friends I can be real with, thank you for pushing me to keep going. There are a million individual contributions to me continuing to be here today, and I am grateful to each one.

Thank you to my doctors at Georgetown University Hospital, Dr. Vikram Nayar and Dr. Deepa Subramaniam, and her oncology nurse Charlotte, all of who spoke to me like a person, not a tumor. Finally, thank you to my amazing doctors at Duke University, and to Lisa Hill-Sutton, my favorite prayer warrior, for sending me to them. I don't know how you deal with brain tumors day after day, but I am so incredibly grateful to each of you. I am especially grateful to Dr. Annick Desjardins for telling me she's proud of me every clean MRI I receive, and to Nurse Rosemary Ketring for cheering me on and taking on my insurance when necessary. They are the best French/Italian duo ever. I am also grateful to Dr. John Kirkpatrick, his magical nuclear symbol cufflinks, and his teams of radiation techs, and to Dr. Henry Friedman for running a brain cancer practice centered around HOPE.

PART ONE

Here's What We're Working With

So Here We Are...

I keep thinking I've heard the worst words in the English language. I thought that when my neurologist told me in 2013 that I had a mass in my brain that "looked like a brain tumor." I thought nothing could be worse than being told my own brain was trying to kill me.

And then I thought that again in 2017 when I was told my cancer had "relapsed" and "metastasized" to my spine. I thought nothing could be worse than being told the tumor I fought so hard to kill was back again trying to take away my ability to walk and go to the bathroom like a grown up.

And then I thought that again about five minutes later when my oncologist, a woman I greatly respect, told me "there are some clinical trials you can look into."

That has to be it, right?

I mean, what could possibly be worse than hearing there are clinical trials for what you're facing. I know what clinical trial means: "We don't know how to fix this, so we're trying some stuff out."

If you've never read notes on a clinical trial, let me explain a little what they look like for brain patients. First, they tell you the name of the drug. This is basically every letter in the English language strung together in a random pattern of 15-18 letters with the maximum number of consonants next to each other leaving you with no possible hope of pronouncing the name of the drug when you talk to your doctor about it. I'm fairly sure that drug companies get bonus points for using Z, V, and Q all in the same name. After that, there is a list of the doctors who are doing the study, the location, other details, and then there's the real fun part.

Study goals.

Now if you've have ever had cancer, your goal, like mine, was "get rid of the cancer and live." However, in brain cancer clinical trials, the goals usually look like this: "six-month progression-free survival" or "to determine the maximum dose safe in adult humans." Six-month progression-free survival? That means, "We are fixin' to try to keep you alive and not growing more tumor for half a year. You get Christmas or Easter, maybe both, depending on when we start you." Dosage determination means, "You are basically a guinea pig for us to figure out how much of this radioactive material we can pump you full of. We might kill you, but you were probably gonna die, anyway—you have a brain tumor."

I didn't take the news well. You don't have to either. But then, you have to decide there is a point at which you are going to stand up, wash your tears off your face (did you know you can cry so much you actually leave a salt-trail on your skin?), and keep going.

I'm hoping sharing my story will help you do just that. Keep going. You've got this.

How This All Started

I ran the Cherry Blossom 10-Miler in Washington D.C. in April 2012. I was 28 years old. I mention that not so you'll know I was young and healthy for context, but because I am a little on the fluffy side. Running 10 miles was quite an accomplishment for me, so I want it in print. If you ever write a memoir, you can choose what you include, too.

The headaches came shortly after the race. By the time we went on our family vacation to the beach in June, I couldn't lie on my stomach to read without my eyes going black so that I couldn't see, and my headaches had turned in to Headaches with a capital H. One night in August, the pain was so overwhelming that, as I was lying on the floor crying, my husband, Austin, told me to either go to the ER, or stop complaining. He was tired of me crying about the headaches and taking no action outside of popping Excedrin. Angry with him for being right and cranky because I was in pain, I went to the ER. I thought I definitely had an aneurism or something, but the dismissive ER doctor that night told me I had migraines, prescribed some medications, and basically told me to man up.

The next day, I took the medication the doctor gave me in the morning while I fed the kids breakfast. I was, at that time, homeschooling our 9, 6, and 4-year-old children. The next thing I remember is waking up on the basement floor at 4 p.m. My oldest son smiled and explained that I had gotten "really tired," and he made his siblings do math and reading, but then decided homeschool was too much work, so they watched *Veggie Tales* while eating all the snacks out of the snack cabinet since he wasn't allowed to use the stove. It took me a second to register where I was and to get my bearings on the fact I'd just lost an entire day. After telling him what a great job he did, I asked him why he didn't call his father on my cell phone when they couldn't wake me up. He said, "We didn't want you to get in trouble with Daddy!" Obviously.

After a quick conversation about how if mommy won't get up off the floor we need to call Daddy and/or 911, I decided never to take the migraine medicine again—at least not if my kids were around. The next few months were miserable as I not only felt progressively worse, but emotionally I beat myself to a pulp for not being able to handle the pain. People have migraines and keep going; I felt like I was shutting down. By around 4 p.m. each day, I was lying in near-tears on the sofa with a cold washcloth on my eyes. Waking in the morning and sitting up felt like crashing into a brick wall. I felt tired and woozy, and most of all, I felt pain. Lots and lots of pain.

Shortly after New Year's Day—nearly five months after my ER visit—I fainted in the hallway while helping my kids get ready for an early morning hockey game. Luckily, my husband was there and took over. I spent the next week in bed with debilitating head pain waiting to see a neurologist because obviously this whole "migraine" thing wasn't working out for me. At this point, however, I was fairly convinced these weren't migraines and I was actually dying because my brain was rotting away inside my head, or I had some kind of a parasite that had grown to the size of a hamster and was running around inside my skull.

Now, I feel like we should pause and talk about doctors. There are some crappy and dismissive doctors out there. Whether that's because they really don't care, think they're right, or are jaded by years of drug-seeking patients; they will send you away and brush you off. A lot of people, especially in the ER, seek medication by claiming headaches. I understand why doctors shoot shade and side-eye people who show up like that. Conversely, there are some amazing, compassionate, attentive doctors. Dr. Sheila Myers, the neurologist I was able to get in to see after my week in bed, was one of those amazing people who clearly went into medicine because she cares deeply about the people she serves. As I explained, tearfully, how I didn't even feel like myself anymore, she smiled and assured me that migraines aren't just headaches, and while she was going to run a few tests to rule out any other issues, if it was migraines, she was going to work with me to find a lifestyle and medicine regime that helped me reclaim my life. We could do this together.

Hope is a powerful thing.

Dr. Meyers sent me in for an MRI and MRA to rule out possible blood clots or physical issues with my neck and head. I have a family history of strokes and pulmonary embolisms, so this made a lot of sense. It was a Thursday, and it was a weird procedure because the MRI technician pulled me out and told me we didn't need to do the contrast MRI or the MRA. She was all set with the scans she needed. I wasn't going to argue. The fewer tests we needed, the better—right? An hour after the test, Dr. Myers called—and I missed it.

Another note about doctors: if you're waiting for test results, trust me when I tell you that you do *not* want them to call you. If they call you ASAP, it's because something is not right. Around 5 p.m., just before her practice closed for the night, I returned Dr. Myers' call. She explained in that same calm, compassionate way that I had a mass in the back part of my brain. She thought it was an ependymoma or a subependymoma, which I asked her to spell. She recommended surgeons at Georgetown and UVA and said she would be happy to get me a referral to Johns Hopkins, if I wanted one. I thanked her for her time and hung up the phone.

I was sitting on my bedroom floor next to the door. My doorbell rang as we hung up and the very adorable Irish guy who always calls me beautiful had come to deliver my groceries. My husband asked me not to drive until we sorted my head out, and I liked being told I was pretty in an Irish accent, so this all worked for me. My husband poked his head in to confirm I'd heard the doorbell and, as I set the phone down, I looked up at him and burst into tears.

Sometimes, you don't have to tell someone the words because they already know.

After Austin was told he was beautiful in an Irish accent—because my man the delivery guy works for tips, you know—he came back and cradled me in his arms while I explained everything the doctor had told me. I don't think there has ever been a better husband in the history of the world because as my thoughts became clearer and less foggy, I explained to my sweet, agnostic Jewish husband that we were going to take 24 hours to be sad and angry and then we were going to trust God and have faith.

And do you know that man got on my crazy train and took it all the way to the station with me? I love him.

A lot.

Treatment (Part the First)

I am a gigantic pain in the butt, and if you ever have to face cancer, especially brain cancer, I want you to be a gigantic pain in the butt, too. You have the right to get multiple opinions, you have the right to seek out the BEST possible care you can get/afford/insurance will cover, and you have the right to take or leave what other people consider to be "the best." It is my understanding that your outcomes for brain cancer are better when you go to an actual brain tumor center and those are a little harder to get to than your local hospital. However, your outcomes are also better when you trust and feel comfortable with the people that you are working with. This includes making doctors work together that don't want to. You know why? Because just like Christmas when your parents are divorced, this is about you, not about their feelings. That's right, you get to be a pain in the butt because you have cancer in your brain. Draw from that whatever conclusions about me you'd like.

If they made it through residency, they can man up their snowflake feelings if you need them to.

Let's back up. After I received the call informing me that there was some kind of a blob growing in my brain, I needed to get that thing out. This meant finding someone I trusted enough to cut open my head and root around in what is unquestionably the best part of me. Some of you have killer legs or a pretty face, some of you might have a beautiful body—I've only ever been intelligent. This cancer was literally attacking the core of who I am. I know many breast cancer patients who have undergone mastectomies who feel they have lost their womanliness, and I felt I was being attacked in a very similar way. That's a very scary thing.

Another scary thing is Google. While I quickly got the records and appointments I needed, I still had some waiting to do. I made a bad decision to use Google, WebMD, and all the other fantastic online resources to gather information for something I didn't even have a firm diagnosis on yet. The thing about that, especially with brain tumors, is the numbers aren't good. Sitting up in the middle of the night wrapped in a blanket and staring at a blue screen in the dark, I remember reading paper after paper, statistic after statistic, and feeling my whole body go cold. Luckily, I had lots of people loving me through the interim and I was able to remind myself that even if a type of tumor had a two percent survival rate, I was available to be that two percent. It's a tough job, but somebody's got to do it. I think in the age of social media and the internet, it's a difficult thing to balance being informed and empowered as a patient or caregiver and not being overwhelmed by medical opinions, statistics, and making yourself a dead number walking. I don't really have a good way to guide you on that idea, everyone has to find their own balance of information and blissful ignorance, but I do know that you need to remember that even when you see statistics, you're not one yet.

I met Doctor Vikram Nayar on my first visit to Georgetown University Medical Center. Waiting in a room with people who you could look like in the future is scary. We tried to develop stories to keep our minds off the fact that these people were probably now disabled due to surgeries very similar to the one I was about to undergo. My husband and I played a game of "Guess the Diagnosis" over text messages, while trying not to laugh at what we each came up with, to keep our minds off the fact I was possibly going to be a 30-year-old with a walker in the near future.

We were called back into the treatment room where we sat anxiously waiting for the doctor to tell us more about what we already knew. Dr. Nayar threw me off when he walked into the room. I think I was expecting someone old who looked more like Albert Einstein. I have no actual reason for that, I had simply decided neurosurgery was where you ended up when you'd been a doctor for a long time and they trusted you around the brains. Dr. Nayar instead was a young, handsome guy with hair like McDreamy from Grey's Anatomy and a well-tailored suit under his white coat. His warmth and calm directness were assuring to me. Obviously, this needed to come out, and he felt he could do a good job, but we'd need better scans than the ones from my local hospital. We went to check out, but as we did, Dr. Nayar's assistant stopped us and said due to my hydrocephalus (that's fluid stuck in your brain making a big, uncomfortable bubble), they didn't feel it was best to let me go anywhere, and they'd be admitting me to the neurology unit of the hospital via the ER.

Well that certainly escalated quickly.

The ER at Georgetown isn't very big, and since I wasn't having a major episode, they put me on a gurney in the hallway. I was smiling and joking with my husband (humor helps, use it) and several doctors flashed weird looks in passing. Finally, one of them stopped and asked me what I was doing in the ER. "I have a brain tumor," I responded.

I think it was the first time I'd said it just like that and I felt my body tremble. I thought about crying. The doctor's face betrayed his thoughts for half a second—most doctors have read WebMD before, too—and then he patted my knee and told me, "You're in the perfect place. At Georgetown, we find problems and fix problems." That sounded simple enough! We'd identified the problem—there was a thing growing inside my brain—and now they were going to take it out and fix it. Easy peasy lemon squeezy.

We were finally admitted to the hospital, and Austin's work was absolutely amazing. He'd taken the morning off to go to the appointment with me but hadn't been ready to tell anyone the whole truth until we knew more. When he called to tell his boss what was happening, he was told to take all the time he needed and not to worry about vacation days because they would make sure we were taken care of while he took care of me. I don't think we could have made it through this process if his work hadn't been so flexible and accommodating. From making sure he knew his job would be there to FedEx-ing a Wi-Fi hot spot overnight so that he could work remotely while I was being treated, my husband's employer was the model of how I think every workplace should be for people facing hardships. They also allegedly sent lunch the day of my surgery, but I was asleep for that. I heard it was tasty, though.

The stay at Georgetown was fairly uneventful. I took a lot of phone calls and texts from friends and family, and I adjusted to the idea that everything happening was, in fact, happening and not just a nightmare. My favorite nurse, Grace, popped in and out asking if I wanted anything for my pain. I'd smile and tell her I was dealing with it just fine. I think I was a little weird for their typical patient. The worst part of my stay was the full brain, full spine MRI they gave me in the middle of the night. Georgetown's imaging center works 24/7, but most of the daytime patients are appointments or emergency patients, so I got the next open spot for a two-hour MRI, which was at 3:00 in the blessed morning. In the meantime, we had lots of time to think about what we were going to do and to try to stay calm—in the hallway of an emergency room where everyone could see us.

You know, no pressure.

A Few Thoughts on MRIs

MRIs (Magnetic Resonance Imaging) are to brain patients what finger sticks are to diabetics. Until they come up with see-through spines and heads, you need MRIs to know what's going on. While they do have "open" MRIs in a few hospitals, generally you get what I lovingly refer to as "the tiny plastic coffin." Some people (Hi, mom!) are so afraid of MRI they have to be blindfolded and given sedatives to get them in the tube for even a 15-minute knee scan. A full brain, full spine MRI with and without contrast can take hours. Luckily for me, I find my mental happy place pretty easily. I've found that playing mind games with myself is really helpful: I sing my times tables, go through capitals of the world, and pray or meditate. I can't quite imagine I'm at the beach; those screeching noises don't allow for much imagination, but I stay pretty chill.

My MRI that first night at Georgetown, however, was about all I could take. I was roused from bed and wheeled out of the room around 2 or 3 in the morning and got the grumpiest MRI tech ever. At Georgetown, they offer headphones that can go in the scanner. It's nice to have music while in the scan, but instead of asking me what I'd like to listen to, I got leftover NPR from the last patient featuring two hours of commentary on why Hilary Clinton should be our next president. (Note: A friend of mine has a heart condition typically found in children, so she gets her MRIs at Children's Hospital and they play movies for her. *Movies!* I get very jealous about that.) (Another note: I worked for years for a Republican.) (One last note: Who actually *enjoys* NPR?)

I felt like brain cancer was enough, and I should not have to suffer this additional indignity, but I made it through. This is a story of overcoming, you guys, and if I can overcome two hours of liberal commentary, you can overcome, too.

I've learned from my many, *many* MRIs that you can ask for what you need. For example, I don't like my techs to check on me between tests. It wastes time, it doesn't calm me down, and I just want out, so I tell them up front this isn't my first rodeo and promise if I need them, I'll squeeze the "freak out ball" they give you to call them. I'm not sure this is scientifically accurate, but I feel I save fifteen minutes in the tiny plastic coffin by not having them say, "How are you doing? This next test will be two minutes," between every single scan. If something helps you, or you just want to sleep, or you need to be talked to, tell them what you need. People can't read minds, so be up front about how they can help you. I've found generally people in medicine do want to help, even if they're cranky.

Telling the Kids

Before you have children, you get very little training in the stuff that's actually going to make an impact on their lives. None of my children remember my ability to bathe them without wetting their belly button the first week of their lives, but I guarantee they all remember being told their mom was sick and needed brain surgery.

How do you break the news about something so overwhelming you don't even have a grasp on it? How do you maintain honesty with your children, because that's always been a priority to us, but not scare them to the point where they cannot function? How do you look into their sweet faces and not break down into tears because the thought of them growing up like a Disney movie without a mom is completely heartbreaking?

It's actually really easy—you make your husband do it.

That's right, I totally chickened out. I let Austin take the kids into a family meeting while I sat upstairs and waited. He told them I had something growing inside my brain that needed to be taken out, we were getting the best doctors, and they were going to take good care of me. He told them I was going to be sick for a long time, and they could help me get better by being patient with me and good for grandma, who was going to take care of them until I was better. Then he brought them upstairs to hug me and I tried to hold it together in spite of their tear-stained faces. I told them how brave they were, how they could pray for me, and how we could trust God had a good plan for our family, even if we didn't like it.

Even though I made Austin break the news to the kids, I learned a lot of things from the experience. It's not like you tell your children and then that's it, they get it and they move on. They continue to have questions, emotional responses, and fears throughout the duration of your illness, and even after. While they don't get nervous to the extent that I do, my children still get anxiety when I go for an MRI, just like I do. I try not to tell them what I'm going in for too far ahead of time, but at this point—they're older and not dumb—they know if I'm taking a half-day off from life, I'm probably going to get an MRI. You can't hide life from your kids, and you really shouldn't try. You're teaching them how to live, be grown-ups, and face scary things. It's more important they see you doing that than see you eating broccoli on the regular, in my opinion.

I think we've had some wins and some losses in how we handled this situation with my children. Gathering them together and telling them a standard, basic message together was a win. It's good if all of your kids, heck, all of your family, is working off a standard set of facts and information. After that, though, we divided and conquered based on each child's needs. What I mean by is we didn't have open Q&A with all three of our children sitting there to hear the answers. The reason is obvious to anyone with children: we have three kids— all completely different people. Our oldest, Riley, who was 9, wanted to know everything there was to know. Riley is, by nature, a highly inquisitive type-A personality. He wanted to know what brain tumors were, if there were survival rates, where my doctors went to college, and what their board scores were. He wanted to see YouTube videos of craniotomies to the posterior fossa and wondered if he could be in the operating room while they were doing it. Our middle child, Logan, is very sensitive and anxious by nature. He was 7 and had one question. He crawled into my lap after Austin told him about my illness, wrapped his arms around me, told me he loved me, and asked with tear-filled eyes if he "had to know anything else." I told him he didn't have to ask any other questions and we wouldn't tell him things if he didn't want to know. My youngest, Savannah, was a few days away from turning 5. She wanted to know if they got to stay at Grammy's house the whole time, or if Grammy was going to stay at our house because Grammy has dogs and she likes dogs. If she had to go to Grammy's house, though, she needed to pack her favorite pillow. Oh, also, did I know that when I went for surgery, they got to go to Uncle Kevin's? So much excitement!

We tried to anticipate some of the things we thought would upset the kids and to deal with them before they became huge issues. Logan twirled my hair around his finger for comfort, so I kept a long lock of it for him, and it's still in his bedside table five years later. We missed anticipating how sad he'd get about the food. People were kind and brought dinner for my family for a long time, but didn't always look at what other people had brought (this isn't a complaint, it's just part of my story) and apparently one day my mom opened the fifth baked pasta dish in a row and Logan cried asking if they were ever going to have food that wasn't mixed together again. He's always been a personal space kind of kid, and he actually hugged a woman who brought fried chicken one night because the food wasn't touching each other. Logan never hugs people—so this was a huge deal. When I am able to return the favor and take people dinner, I now always try to take something that isn't a casserole.

Another thing we failed to anticipate was how completely idiotic the adults surrounding our children could be. Yes, I said idiotic, and no, I'm not sorry, and I'm not tempering that with a "but I understand." Flat out—if you know a child is in the middle of a crisis, DO NOT ASK THE CHILD FOR INFORMATION. It is not the job of a child to answer questions about their parent's health. It is not the job of a child to answer questions about treatment. It is not the job of a child to have to talk about something so intensely painful and scary in a public place. If you are in a position to interact with a child in a difficult situation, the *only* thing you should say, and not in front of other children, is "Hey, I'm sorry this is happening, and if you ever want to talk, I'm here." You should then promptly change the subject to Power Rangers, chocolate cake, or Harry Potter. Don't put a child in a situation where they're going to cry in front of everyone, and that includes prying for information before praying. "Logan, is there anything special we should pray for mommy about? Has she gotten any new information? Is she sick from the medicine?" Don't put a child in a situation where they feel like they're being interrogated by a group of adults for information on something that feels very intimate and personal to them.

And, for the love of crepes, *don't* assume the kids know everything. When we were deciding whether or not to go to Duke University for radiation, I mentioned it online and people took that as free license to ask my kids whether or not they were moving to Durham. The number of people who took it upon themselves to make this situation harder for my children was astonishing. I've forgiven these people, but I'm still mad at the situation happening, and I definitely don't want it to happen to other children facing a similar situation.

A fairly famous pop-psychologist says something along the lines of don't make children feel powerless by making them deal with adult issues.

We had to figure out a way to give them that power back. What we ended up doing was giving our children permission to do something we hadn't ever considered before, and that was to be self-protecting and rude. If an adult asked them a line of questions about me, or even one question about me, and they didn't want to answer, they had our permission to say, "You can ask my grandma/dad/whatever adult they were with." If the adult continued to question them, and yes, that happened, they had our permission to say, "You are making me uncomfortable and I don't want to talk to you," and walk away. However you want to do it, empower your children to handle the people around them so they don't have to endure any additional pain because of adults who want information. Other kids are incredibly intuitive at handling these things when left to their own devices. I remember watching Savannah with a friend one day, and the little girl said, "Hey, Savannah, your mommy is sick?" and Savannah responded, "Yeah, she's really sick." The little girl gave her a hug and said, "I'm sorry. Let's play dolls now."

Try that. It's pretty perfect.

Second Opinions

A few hours after my NPR experience, Dr. Nayar came into my hospital room to go over my new fancy MRI imaging and what he thought our course of action should be. It's strange to have serious conversations with people when the back portion of you is flapping in the breeze—thank you hospital gowns. Dr. Nayar discussed the risk of surgery, his approach, and how long he thought surgery would take, and then told me I could choose radiation and not surgery, or to do nothing. I would die, obviously, if we did nothing, but I had choices. As crazy as it sounds, his offering me choices meant so much to me. They were dumb choices—the amount of radiation I'd need to make a dent in a tumor the size of the citrus fruit I'd grown was practically lethal, and dying slowly of a balloon of spinal fluid in my brain would be painful and counterproductive to my goal of being around for my children— but Dr. Nayar offering options gave me back some sense of control in a situation where I was very much out of control. We booked my surgery for the next Wednesday, and he agreed to let me go home until then as long as I came back if I developed any new symptoms.

Georgetown had been amazing. They'd called an emergency tumor board, bumped other surgeries, and really gone out of their way to make sure they could help me as soon as possible. We felt really good about Georgetown, the nursing staff, and Dr. Nayar.

Since we'd already reached our per-person maximum on my insurance, it didn't really matter if I checked out of the hospital, but we had a consultation at Johns Hopkins on Thursday, and we definitely wanted to get a second opinion. I prayed really hard God would make it abundantly clear where I was supposed to go for surgery, and I had high hopes we'd know what was right. For those of you who aren't aware, Johns Hopkins University is amazing and according to a lot of our friends, I should "definitely want to go to JHU" over Georgetown. I think no matter what, if you have time for a second opinion, you should get one, so off to Baltimore we went.

Spoiler Alert: Hopkins was a nightmare for me. Thanks for the clarity, God! (PS- It is awesome for a lot of people, please don't sue me, okay?)

First of all, Baltimore, Maryland, is the official sponsor of potholes that could eat a Hyundai Elantra, which is what we had driven up in, and the idea of being driven home after major brain surgery through the streets of Charm City did not appeal to me. When we walked into Hopkins, I was overwhelmed by the size of the place, and, while taking it in, a security guard yelled at me to know where I was going. We lined up at the elevators with a crowd of people, and even with six elevators, it took three rotations to get everyone in. We shared an elevator with a man in a gurney moaning in horrible pain whose face was covered by a blanket.

When we finally arrived in neurosurgery, giant overhead deli-counter style signs indicated in red lights whose turn it was to the see doctors. "Now Serving B18" isn't quite what I was looking for in health care. I walked up to the counter to check in and learned that despite the lengthy process I had gone through before being told I qualified for an appointment—sending in information from my neurologist, radiologist, MRI scans, insurance forms, and a full personal health background—Hopkins didn't have my information on file and wasn't sure they could see me today.

Say what?

After pulling up everything on our iPhones we could, we were told the neurosurgeon would, in fact, see us. The doctor I saw has wonderful online reviews and is world-renowned. I am sure he is fantastic, and he might even be the perfect doctor for you, but he was not for me.

First, his resident walked in and did the standard neurological exam, which I call the trained monkey exam, and asked me about my background. Then the doctor waltzed in saying he had hopes only for good things for me—a long life and a future. He said my Georgetown MRI was inadequate and I'd need new scans, which would take a week to schedule, and then he'd develop a plan and meet with the brain tumor board, which would be another week. Finally, he'd get his team together and check his speaking schedule—he had something coming up in China—so we were looking at April or May for my surgery. In the course of this, it came up that he hadn't even looked at my scans before seeing me. He just assumed they weren't good enough and I would need new ones. (Note: I've learned every hospital on earth "has the best MRI in the world," which is really them letting you know they want to bill your insurance for scans, if we're being super honest.)

Austin jumped in and asked about the hydrocephalus that had Georgetown so concerned they'd moved everything around to fit me in as soon as they could safely plan the surgery. The Hopkins doctor assured me they could just "pop in a shunt." He'd done hundreds of this type of surgery and I didn't need to worry about anything since he knew what was right for me. This is a good time to mention how important it is to take someone to your appointments with you. Sometimes there's so much information, or such a weird change in approach, it can take a moment for your brain to wrap around it. It's especially great if the person you're taking with you tends to be overly technical and removed from immediate emotional responses. Am I telling you that you *have* to take a software engineer (or really, engineer of any kind) with you? No, but they do an excellent job, from my personal experience.

When we left the appointment, I was ready to cry again. This was all wrong. I was a number to these people, and not someone who was involved in the decision-making process. They had taken away the power Dr. Nayar had given me in explaining my options. I called my dear friend Lisa, who has a background in brain tumors, and explained my misgivings. Lisa had a very strong opinion that with brain tumors you either get it out, or you biopsy it immediately, but you don't let it keep growing. She's known people who were told their tumor was benign and it ended up being deadly. She also assured me that while Hopkins is a great name in tumor care, if Georgetown wanted to make me a priority and I felt at peace, then she's Catholic and liked them better anyway. Lisa also brought me steak before my surgery. She's fully awesome.

So, we decided to forget Hopkins, set our calendars for February 5, and by the time we arrived home, we knew confidently we were going for the Georgetown plan.

And then Austin realized he'd left his laptop at JHU, two hours away. I did ask God to make it abundantly clear where we were supposed to go for surgery, and I can safely say Hopkins was not it.

Turning Your Friends
into Professionals

I think to properly cover everyone in my life who helped me make it through this process I'd probably have to write this chapter twice. The people who stepped into my life and my family's life to help us are innumerable and sometimes even anonymous. I literally had my breath taken away by the kindness of friends, neighbors, and even strangers who were moved to help my family make it through this process. However, I am going to try to sum up the professional friends you will need to get you through cancer, or really, any kind of a traumatic life event.

One: The Experienced Advocate
First and foremost, if you can find a friend who is something of a subject matter expert, or who is simply not afraid of medical issues and big words, they will be invaluable to you. My friend Lisa, who I'd met years before through a parenting group, ended up being the person I knew

was safe to go to when I got scary news or wasn't sure what to think. Lisa was married to a man who had a Glioblastoma Multiforme, the worst possible brain diagnosis you can receive. Lisa fought for him, losing everything in the process, and became such an expert the doctors she worked with to save her husband gave her a white coat of her own. Now, while I think I would run from that pain and never want to relive it, Lisa has stayed an advocate for brain tumor patients and relives the loss of her first husband again and again, helping people like me to navigate the scary waters of this type of diagnosis. It was Lisa who connected me with the amazing doctors at Duke; Lisa who I could ask questions like, "What do I do if the radiation is making me burp metal," and Lisa who was up at 3 a.m. to pray with me or for me when I was up with anxiety.

Two: The Professional Organizer

Second, but only by a little bit, if you have a friend who is type A-plus and offers to take over your family, say yes to that blessing. My darling friend Sheri, already homeschooling and running her family of six, organized meals, playdates, and rides for my children to the point I did not cook a meal until nine months after surgery. I don't know how she did it, but I am eternally grateful. When people had questions about what my family needed, how I was doing, or if we had any allergies, they went to her and she served as a hub of information instead of having 300 people calling my mom Lydia, or Austin.

Third: The Village

Third is everybody else, and again, third, but only by a little bit. My surgery was scheduled for February 5, but my daughter's birthday was February 13. When my friends learned I would be home for the weekend before my surgery, they got on my Pinterest board and made my daughter's birthday party happen pin for pin. Even the ones I probably never would have actually gotten to. They organized a group of women to come and sing hymns and pray with me on Tuesday night. They showed up with gifts for the kids, socks for the hospital, prayer shawls, afghans, and new pajamas. The showered us with cards and prayers and notes from monasteries praying for our family. They had masses said for us, they had missionaries add us to prayer lists in Africa, Asia, and South America—my friends circled the globe to show us how loved and surrounded we were by people who cared. I have never felt so loved or so surrounded by people in my whole life, and it was an incredible feeling. I will never be able to adequately thank everyone in my life who stood in the gap for my family or who surrounded me with love I did not deserve, whether in the form of cards, prayers, gifts, or food. However, I take every opportunity I can to pay that love forward whenever I can.

Ultimately, it takes a village for you to successfully get through any kind of a crisis. My sister-in-law, Jordana, who I love only slightly less than my husband, became a de facto communications manager for his whole side of the family. I put the Mayhughs, the lovely couple who run my small group at church, in charge of informing everyone there of my second diagnosis. Lisa and Sheri ran a team of "cheerleaders" online, passing information weekly. Austin or I could send one email update to this core group of people and that way everyone knew who to go to for information about how I was doing—and it wasn't us. You can really only tell the same story so many times before you go crazy, so we outsourced.

You're also going to find that you have friends with a variety of different talents, and that you need to have all of those talents at different times. You need Shavaun to dance in the church parking lot with you because she is so effervescently excited about what God's going to do. You need Jennifer to listen to you when you want someone to say all the curse words and tell you this is not acceptable and they're angry at this situation with you. You need Kris to say, "Do you wanna talk about it? Because if not, I have a great story about spraining my thumb on a bra."

You need people to organize, to support, to have your kids on days when they need to just get away. You need a medical sounding board who isn't afraid of pictures of things like infections on your skin and big words that lead to even bigger words on WebMD. If you were to actually put out a Monster.com list for all the people you need to "hire" to get you through a crisis, the list would be extensive, and you'd probably have to pay for health insurance for them because you'd be at least a medium-sized corporation.

Luckily, it seems like people step up for these roles, and if you're really lucky, one day you'll get to be there for someone else, too, and you'll be even better at it for having had the people in your life who kept you going.

I'm Not Driving This Vehicle

I don't like airplanes. That might seem a little out of left-field, but it's important for you to know that about me to understand what I'm about to tell you. I don't like airplanes because I am putting my life and the lives of my family into the control of some random dude I've never met who's locked behind a thick metal door. I don't know if he slept well the night before, or if he got an A in aviation or was more of a "C's get degrees" type of guy. I would be much happier if I was flying the plane because I know I want to get there safely, and I know my own capabilities. Unfortunately for me, I don't get to be in control of the airplane because I don't happen to have a commercial pilot's license. Surrendering control when there are so many unknowns is really hard for me—and it applies in many areas of my life.

Control was an interesting teeter-totter during my original diagnosis. On the one hand, I had given the situation over to God when I informed Austin we were getting on my "crazy train" and having complete faith and trust in God's plan for my life. However, giving up the situation to God did not mean I had to give up being involved in what was happening.

Because God had the situation under control, I didn't have to fear what the outcome would be, but that didn't mean I signed off from being engaged in what was happening. I still sought out second opinions, I still made decisions, I still valued being told I had choices, and I very, very much did not want to let this brain tumor take anything from me. I think that was why being told I had choices was important. If I chose to have brain surgery, then I was not sitting idly by and allowing the tumor to slowly choke out my life. If I chose to go to Georgetown, then I was selecting my surgeon and not simply taking what was offered to me as a passenger in a car my doctors were driving while I sat in the back seat blindfolded.

I extended that to a lot of other things that were important to me, too. For example, I chose to donate my hair the night before surgery. The pre-surgery team told me they could shave portions of my head, but I didn't want the brain tumor to take my hair, so I gave it away. I'd always wanted to donate my hair, but every time it got past a certain length, it drove me insane. I could never get it long enough to donate the required length and still have some left. Shaving my head meant I had enough length and didn't have to worry about having any left.

The owner of the salon I go to kindly came to my house to shave my head. I worried about doing it in the salon since I didn't want a ton of people asking questions or demanding to know what I was thinking cutting off my very long, naturally blonde hair. I was worried I would cry, but I actually loved feeling my short stubble—it felt nice on my scalp. As a bonus, I got to sugar scrub my head the night before surgery, which felt amazing. If you have to go bald, treat yourself to a sugar scrub on your scalp. It feels so nice, and it's not something you can do when your head is covered with hair!

For me, it was important to let God have the situation while I remained engaged in decisions I could make. I was in control of what I could be in control of and God was in control of the rest. If that helps you, then take the reins on anything you can and know you made the choice, for example, to help out a kid with cancer who now has your hair. Keeping a grasp on what you can control and giving up the things you can't is a healthy way to deal with a situation that could easily make you mentally spiral out of control if you tried to manage everything… because you simply can't do it.

So, Then There Was Surgery

The night before my surgery was a Tuesday. We had family dinner with my children, and then they got to go and spend the night with their Uncle Kevin, who had taken the day off on Wednesday to be emotionally available to them. Knowing they were excited to get such a special treat—a mid-week sleepover with their Uncle!—helped me to say goodbye with a smile on my face.

And then I sat on the floor inside my front door and wept. My kids were still so little. Would they remember anything I'd taught them? Would my daughter even remember me? Had I said goodbye forever, or was it temporary? Tomorrow someone was going to cut my head open and I didn't know which of the potential negatives I'd be left with— paralysis, memory issues, death. What had I just done? Had I sent my children happily away on the last night of my life?

Luckily, the aforementioned friends scheduled an in-home prayer and praise session. People started showing up just when I needed them.

A big crowd of about thirty women crammed into my townhouse. People said they were angry, sad, scared, but ultimately, that they had faith. We cried. We sang. We hugged. I felt better having these sweet women surround me and feel things with me. My husband stood behind me the whole time. I'm not sure quite what he or his sister, also Jewish, who'd flown in from California to be a support for Austin, thought about all this. I hope they felt all the love and faith and how much it lifted me up.

We probably would've gone all night, but the hairstylist showed up to shave my head, and with final hugs and kisses, everyone headed out. They'd also planned a "prayer party" for me the next day (because a vigil sounded like I was dying) and had people praying in 15-minute increments starting at 5 a.m. when I'd head out for the hospital. Knowing they were doing that really gave me tremendous hope and peace.

Prep for surgery was basic. After having my head shaved, I showered in antibacterial soap and took off my nail polish. Not being allowed to use any deodorant or lotion was hard for me—I like to smell pretty, and I have *super* dry skin, so my skin felt tight and uncomfortable, but I survived. Austin and I talked late into the night and then, when he fell asleep, I wrote him notes. Dr. Nayar said my surgery would take four to eight hours. We told people it would take eight to ten hours so they wouldn't worry if I took a little longer. I wrote Austin one note per hour, and decided to do 13, in case something went wonky. I included a just-in-case note for him letting him know I'd already given a pastor friend instructions on how to conduct my funeral and I'd picked out a place to be buried so he wouldn't have to figure anything out. This was partly me trying to cling desperately to what little control I could retain, and part me not wanting to leave my funeral in the hands of my non-practicing Jewish husband. The other notes were funny or touching, reminding him of funny things from our time dating, silly jokes, and reasons that I loved him. I even included a "pin the scalpel on the brain" game from pieces I cut out from online clip art. I wanted him to be supported by me, even when I couldn't be there. The surgery was happening to me, but I knew I had the easy part. I got to sleep through the scary part, while Austin waited knowing he couldn't do anything. I would never want to have to do that in reverse.

I didn't sleep much. Letter writing kept me up most of the night and then I had to shower again in antibacterial soap before heading to the hospital. I figured it was okay if I was super-tired because I'd get to spend the next several hours in a blissful state of medication-induced slumber.

Once we arrived at the hospital, I shocked Dr. Nayar with my freshly bald head and scared the nurses who came to give me "something to calm me down" because they quickly realized I was already calm. Austin gave me a kiss goodbye and headed back to wait with my family. I thought I might completely freak out having to give him what could be a last kiss goodbye. While we were both misty, neither of us cried, and I honestly felt numb emotionally at that point, which made my nurses think I was incredibly calm and composed. It was more like I was watching what was happening to me than really living it.

My uncle had driven up from Charlotte. He's a surgeon, and I am sure that having someone to interpret medical speak for my family was helpful. My sister-in-law was there for Austin, and my parents were there, as well. My mom was like a guardian angel behind us during this entire process—doing whatever had to be done while supporting my children, Austin, and me. She's more forcefully opinionated than an angel, but I know that's because she didn't want me to starve to death after surgery. I heard my family kept the entire waiting room in stitches playing Operation, Cranium, and Headbands. That's right, folks. My family brought brain-surgery-themed games to entertain them while they waited for me. I told you humor goes a long way to help you get through this, and I meant it.

I remember being disappointed with the operating room. There was no glass-walled gallery for people to watch my surgery like there is on all the doctor shows on TV. It was just a sterile-looking white room that held way more blue people in masks than I thought there should be. It was like a clown car of doctors and nurses. Georgetown is a teaching hospital, and, as I mentioned, I try to be a good sport. So when the anesthesiology student couldn't get the large IV needle into my vein for surgery, I tried to encourage her by telling her it was no big deal because she'd numbed my arm first and everything was going to be fine. She'd get it the second time. A man I assumed to be the head anesthesia guy didn't give her a chance to do it twice since she was flustered. As he put in the needle, someone I hadn't met before and never saw again walked in and started talking about what an interesting case I was and how you didn't generally see these. Dr. Nayar gave a death stare and informed him the patient was still awake. I started to tell him that I didn't mind, I wasn't bothered by people talking about my condition, and as the anesthesia set in, I could hear him say, "But I mind." Then I was asleep.

Thirteen hours later, Austin ran out of notes. This was a shame because I'd really included some fantastic ones. Well, that's not entirely true—he'd run out of notes except my final "Open-If-It-Hits-The-Fan" instructions for what to do if I didn't make it out of surgery. It wasn't nice of me that my 14th note, besides detailing funeral plans, was to remind him I would find a way to haunt him forever if he messed my kids up. I think there was also some mushy stuff in there about how he'd given me such a happy life and I wanted him to be happy in the future. I don't really remember, and luckily, he didn't have to open it. However, I know that running out of notes and realizing the only thing he had left to hold from me was the "In Case of Death" notice was really hard on him. I feel badly about that, but I never would have dreamed that my 4- to 8-hour surgery would turn into a 16-hour marathon.

And Then I Woke Up

Most of what I'm about to tell you is hearsay, because one thing I can tell you for sure is they give you all the good drugs after brain surgery. I remember my uncle the surgeon being at the foot of my bed the morning after my surgery and telling me, "They're going to offer you some medication, and you're going to want to take that," and thinking, "Duh," but being unable to make my mouth convey my sarcasm effectively. I think I tried to nod, realized that was a horrible idea, and stared blankly. I did take the medication and because of that, I don't remember a lot of my first week, but I have heard the stories.

By the time they completed my surgery and closed me up, recovery was closed, so they took me directly to the ICU. Apparently as I was waking up, I heard the surgeon talking to my family and saying something about sixteen hours being a long time to have the brain open, and I groggily said, "Sixteen hours? What took you so long?" Which helped my family know that I was all there—at least mentally. Austin

36

was beyond elated with everything that I did. Moving my fingers and knowing who he was made him feel overcome with relief. It was similar to being a baby again and having people clap and be thrilled with every little sound and gesture you make just because you exist. What made Austin special was he could see through all of the trauma I'd been through to the bigger picture that I was still functional, whereas my sister-in-law, Jordana, cried when she saw me because I was frankenbeast and beyond help or hope of survival. Looking at the pictures, I understand. Whether it was from trauma or steroids, I was swollen everywhere. The back of my head had a six-inch scar sealed with staples, and the top of my head had a drain coming out of a freshly-bored hole. There was a pink baggie of spinal fluid coming out of that drain, and a yellow one coming out of a drain a little further south. I had IVs and blood pressure cuffs, and compression sleeves on both legs to prevent blood clots during the time I was flat and not moving. I had a halo, and not the cute kind you get in the Christmas play, screwed into my scalp. I remember being taken for a CT scan after the surgery with the halo still on and having it hurt like (insert your favorite expletive here) when they pulled me down to align me correctly. I'm pretty sure Jordana had it right on about the frankenbeast, but I'm very thankful that Austin didn't turn tail and run.

It is normal after brain surgery for light and sounds to be LIGHT and SOUNDS. It is also normal after brain surgery for them to put you on massive doses of steroids. This is a fun combination because no matter how you normally treat your family, you will be in a lot of pain with a lot of 'roid rage. Everything that happens ticks you off. I apparently screamed at people for the following things:

- Whispering
- Breathing too loudly
- Touching my bed
- Touching any part of my body

- Walking too loudly
- Chewing gum
- Existing in my presence

Luckily for you, if you're the one being operated on, your family will be happy you didn't kick the bucket. They'll forgive you for being such a wicked jerk. I remember getting a sponge bath and wanting to die. I begged God for death because on top of the pain, the cold and shivering were awful. When they did my surgery, to access the posterior fossa (fancy speak for back of my neck) they had me kneeling. After being in that position for so long, I had giant pressure blisters on my knees and breasts where the weight from my body was being supported for 16 hours. I remember having terrible nightmares and sometimes screaming in my sleep because of the steroids. I remember making deals with nurse Dan, also awesome, that if I could walk around the ward twice, he'd let me take a shower with my mom's help. I believe it took me forty-five minutes to walk about 300 feet, but that shower was the best thing that ever happened to me. (Note: Shaving my head was a genius decision. All the blood and goop coming out of me from the drain in my forehead and the stitches all over me were not stuck in my hair. That would have been way too much for me to deal with, even with my mom there to help.)

While incredibly mad at my family for making noises related to them existing, I also didn't want them to leave me. I couldn't think clearly through the fog of pain and medication and general reaction of my body to what I'd just let them do to me. I needed people to advocate for me and help me remember things and make sure I got the care I needed. Luckily, my mother and my husband were both bad mother shut-your-mouths and were not at all deterred by things like "visiting hours" or "sleep" or "that witchy face the nurse is making at them." One of the night nurses would send them back out to the waiting room fifteen minutes of every hour to check on me, and then they'd sneak right back in. If I woke up and couldn't immediately identify one of them sitting silently and not breathing too loud, I would panic.

A bunch of other things happened that I have no memory of. I'm told I had roommates and one of them even coded and was resuscitated in my presence. We had a birthday dinner for my daughter in the waiting room of the ICU. Allegedly I had a conversation with my friend Gaby about Jehovah's Witnesses and even told her which Bible verses to quote, but I remember none of that.

Not a normal thing that happens, but I blew out veins constantly. I think I have the worst veins on earth. At one point, they tried to put an IV in my foot, which was the most painful thing I think I've had done, and I've given birth unmedicated. They had to bring in a vascular specialist with an ultrasound to put in an IV under my armpit. I'm not sure how many IVs I had, but I know it was a ton. I also remember yelling at a resident who came in one night to check on me. Fun story: when you're recovering from brain surgery, they wake you up from what fitful, steroid-filled sleep you get to shine light in your eyes, ask you questions, and make you squeeze their fingers. One night, a resident had forgotten his regular flashlight and used some kind of mag light keychain and I thought he was burning my eyes out. Again 'roid rage. I don't think I ever saw him again.

When I was moved back to the neuro "step-down," which is the unit between the ICU and home, I got my favorite nurse, Grace, back. The doctors, however, made the mistake of telling me once I was off IV pain meds, I could go home. Let me back up a little. Initially, they told my family to expect I'd be in the ICU for a few weeks, then in the step down for a few weeks, and then they might need to place me in a rehab facility for weeks to months to recover function after such a long surgery right around my brain stem. As previously mentioned, however, I am a stubborn pain in the butt (and my surgeon was amazing). So, after a few days in the ICU, I was up walking and moved to the step down. When they told me I could go home if I could stop the IV pain meds, I told them I was done with the IV pain meds, and I was going to go home.

Grace was smart. She'd come in with oral pain meds and tell me she had the IV meds in her pocket and I could have them. I would refuse, shaking a little inside since I was in incredible pain, but I was more so a stubborn pain in the butt than the pain.

I went home eight days after my marathon surgery.

This stupidity was not due to surgical complications, but my own bad choices.

That Time I Went
Home Too Soon

I really wanted to go home. For anyone that's ever been in a hospital before, you understand. You don't sleep well, you miss your family, the food is horrible, especially if you're like me and had to be on a mechanical soft (read: baby food) diet because the breathing tubes damaged your vocal chords and ability to swallow. While the pre-thickened cranberry juice was amazing, the pureed turkey and canned gravy a la blender was enough to make me want to blow this pop stand.

After stubbornly refusing IV pain meds, I was cleared to go home. I realized this was the worst decision of my life as they helped me into my mother's car. Mid-transfer I wanted to yell that I'd changed my mind. However, I'd worked too hard and denied too many shots of Valium to turn back now, so I laid in the car and cried all the way from Georgetown to my home in Woodbridge, Virginia. It took about an hour, and I could barely move or think by the time we arrived. I don't remember how my mother and husband got me up the stairs of our townhouse, let alone into my bedroom, but I know there was no amount of pain medication that could even touch how awful I was feeling.

Austin was so much more than a rockstar at this point. He set the alarm on his phone for my ridiculous medicine schedule, waking up every few hours all night long to give me steroids, pain medication, muscle relaxers, antibiotics, and I'm not sure what all else. He brought me ice and coaxed me to sip juice or smoothies. He rotated our very afraid children in to see me one at a time so they would not jostle me or jump on me, and he telecommuted at the same time. My mom, also a rock star, took off a semester from school—she'd decided to earn her bachelor's degree—and homeschooled my children, kept them going to scouts and sports, and held them when they cried because their mom, while home, wasn't actually there.

My baby brother, Kevin, whose stats read like an NFL linebacker, is a physical therapist and came to my house as soon as I was home to start working on my legs and arms and sitting up. After a while, my mom or Austin would help me outside to walk. We lived in a townhouse community, and at first, I could walk to the end of our sidewalk, then to the edge of our end-unit home, and eventually I added one townhouse at a time. Before my surgery, I had read about the Race for Hope, which is an annual event in Washington, D.C., to raise money for brain tumors, and I wanted to walk the 5K, even though it would be in the middle of the rest of my treatment, which we still had to figure out. There's that stubbornness of mine, again.

Eventually, my brother started to see me in-clinic, and I'm pretty sure his goal was to pay me back for everything I'd ever done wrong to him. However, I have to say that if you can find a physical therapist that will work with you like he worked with me, you will benefit beyond belief. From making me catch balls (they move so fast!) while standing on balance foam (jerk) to using electrode therapy (ouch) to lessen my post-operative neuropathy, my brother was a miracle worker, and I keep trying to persuade him to write a protocol for brain tumor patients. The work he did was so good that by the time I entered the next phase of my treatment elsewhere, the physical therapists couldn't believe I'd had the surgery I did. I'm eternally grateful for the time, effort, and physical pain he put me through. It was worth every agonizing moment. If you're able to get into physical therapy, take advantage of *every* single workout. They hurt, and they suck, and you might cry, or laugh hysterically—I actually laugh when I'm in really bad pain and a lot of the people at my brother's practice stared at me—but do the work. You'll never regret giving yourself everything you have.

Compulsive Lying

When I got home from my surgery, I turned into a compulsive liar. I lied to everyone. I lied to my friends, my family, my children. I even tried to lie to myself. Here's the thing: people are really good at the initial illness, but most of them want you to get better in a fashion similar to having strep throat. When you have strep, you feel poorly, you go to the doctor, you get antibiotics, and you feel better twenty-four to forty-eight hours later.

It just doesn't work that way with cancer.

Recovery from all the treatment I needed was going to take twelve to eighteen months. That's a long time for people to hear you're still sick. You survived the surgery, and they want to hear that you feel better. You know what a side effect of craniotomies is? Headaches. It's completely possible you're not going to get "better." You could have brain surgery and still have the symptoms that you went in with. You could have brain surgery and have deficits for the rest of your life. You could have brain surgery and feel like death warmed over for weeks, months, even years.

And some people can't handle that.

Even more than that, I don't like to seem weak or feel like I'm failing to meet people's expectations. Recovery was hard. My kids asking, "Are you better today, Mommy?" was hard. Walking down the stairs was hard. When people came to see me, I planned ahead so I would already be down the stairs sitting on the sofa by the time they arrived, so I could pretend I was happy and easily getting around the house. When they left or got chased out by my mom or my husband, I slept for hours to recover from thirty minutes of activity.

I lied when something was wrong, and I had to go back to the ER. I lied by omission when I found something to be happy about and that was the only thing I put on Facebook. I didn't tell people about crawling up the stairs after my first physical therapy appointment with my brother and weeping from exhaustion and pain. I didn't tell people about having a horrible headache and fever and having to go back in to be checked for infection. I didn't tell them about how having a second lumbar puncture in a week gave me a vasovagal reaction and I thought I was dying. (Note: Vasovagal reactions make you feel like you can't breathe. Your heart slows down and your blood pressure bottoms out. Not a good time.) I didn't tell them how after the same lumbar puncture I had to stay two days in the hospital because I lacked sufficient spinal fluid to sit up without vomiting from pain.

I just kept lying—either by omission, or by fakery, or just by choice.

And the thing is, I figured out quickly there are some people who will block you on Facebook if you aren't better on their timeline. And there are some people who don't want to hear about it after they've lost interest. However, there are safe people, too, and they want to know how you are and they are hurt that you're lying. When I ended up back in the ER, for example, it was my husband's first day back at work, so my mother took me in. We had to ask my friend, Sheri, to help with the kids. And when my mom was talking to her on the phone in the ER, I could clearly hear her screaming, "WHY IS THIS THE FIRST TIME I'M HEARING ANYTHING IS WRONG? WE LOVE HER AND CAN'T HELP HER IF SHE DOESN'T TELL US THAT THINGS ARE WRONG!"

Find those people. Don't lie to them. They love you, and they can't help you if you don't tell them that things are wrong. I know it's a balance to try to stay positive—which was important for my own mental state—and stay real but try to find that balance. You don't have to tell everyone everything that is happening, but you should have a few people you can trust so you don't go crazy. It's really important.

Ependymomas

Warning: I'm about to talk medical to you. It's like talking dirty, but less fun and harder to understand. Feel free to skip this chapter if you're not interested.

As I mentioned before, you can't really tell what you're working with in terms of brain tumors until they pop that sucker out and biopsy it. Ependymomas come in grades I-III, unlike some tumors that go to IV. After my tumor was removed, it was confirmed that it was a Grade II Ependymoma. A high grade II. Maybe it was thinking about grade III because it had a mitosis rate of 25% and for grade two they really like that number around 10%—but it wasn't quite "ugly" enough.

That's right, y'all. My tumor was pretty.

The good news about ependymomas is that in adults, they have fairly high five- and ten-year survival rates, especially when compared with glioblastomas, astrocytomas, and other high-grade gliomas. The bad part about ependymomas is they're fairly rare in adults, accounting for only about two percent of adult brain tumors, and because of that they don't know a lot about them. Since little is known, there's a lot of gut work involved in treating them. At the time I was diagnosed, we read a few things that said a grade II ependymoma isn't even cancer. Other sources disagreed. Here's the thing: as with any brain tumor that causes symptoms, there is a large mass growing in a limited space inside your skull and it's trying to kill you. If it walks like a duck and quacks like a duck, then call that sucker a mallard. I call my grade II "brain cancer" because it was trying to kill me. I'm even more dedicated to that analysis since I was told that it would come back. Tumors that come back are definitely trying to kill you, ergo, cancer.

I had a total gross resection of my maybe-cancerous tumor. Rather than that meaning my surgery was disgusting, which it probably was, that means they got the whole thing out. I was told I had a completely clean lumbar puncture, as well, with no trace of cancer cells, although I have since learned that ependymoma cells are notoriously "sticky" and lumbar punctures are a stupid way to try to determine if you have any remaining cells.

Now what?

Well, that's a good question. Some doctors at the time thought radiation wasn't necessary in a total gross resection of an ependymoma. Other doctors thought radiation was completely necessary, even if the tumor was completely removed, unless it was a grade I. What was definitely known is that ependymomas are notorious for not responding to chemotherapy, so recurrences aren't good since your body can only stand so much radiation, and it is the only thing that really works on ependymomas besides surgery.

Luckily, science changes.

If you need more information on ependymomas, I recommend the Collaborative Ependymoma Research Network (CERN). Their publications are obviously written by doctors (read: don't expect to glean lots of hope and sunshine from it), but they do have the most up-to-date information you're going to find. www.cern-foundation.org.

As for me, since nobody really knew for sure what they should do, we made it our mission to again find doctors we were comfortable with and made us a part of the process, rather than spectators watching my life happen around me.

Figuring Out What's Next

A fun part about brain tumors is that in addition to having someone root around in your head, you then get to continue making decisions while you're high as a kite, tired, and hurting. I, for example, needed to make decisions about follow-up care. We were told if we did nothing, we could expect the tumor to come back in nine to eighteen months. We were told that radiation could probably buy me seven to ten years. I laughed at the idea that my life was now being defined in terms of prison sentences. "I'm doing seven to ten for ependymoma." Usually you get that kind of a prison term for a weapons charge, but I was going to be held hostage by my diagnosis for that length of time.

(Note: Unlike other types of cancer, brain isn't considered to be "in remission" until year ten, and I've read stories of recurrence past that.)

So, if you're a "good patient," you get handed off to another team member in the same place you started, and you get your treatment and that's it. We tried really hard to make ourselves feel good about the radiation oncology team where we started, but it just never clicked for us. One good thing that happened from those visits, though, was that we found out my spirit animal.

Me: "I just don't understand how people missed this for so long."

Doctor: "Well in medical school, they teach us that when you hear "neigh" you should think horse, not zebra. You're a zebra."

When I posted that conversation on Facebook (and how could you not, it's hilarious), I had a friend angrily reply that I better call that doctor back and inform him that I am *not* a zebra, I'm a "Magical Effing Unicorn."

And so, my spirit animal was born, and people started sending me unicorn everything. I have a better collection of unicorns than an 11-year-old girl at a Lisa Frank convention. True Story.

So, if we weren't happy where we started off, where did we go? Remember my friend Lisa, who lost her first husband to a glioblastoma? She referred us to Duke's Robert Preston Tisch Brain Tumor Center and Dr. Henry Friedman. Dr. Friedman is fully awesome, and really, why would you see anyone who isn't? How fully awesome is he? If you look him up on YouTube, you can watch him give interviews on places like *60 Minutes* and CNN in his signature Duke hoodie and sneakers. He doesn't have time to get dressed up to go on CNN because he's too busy curing cancer. In our initial phone call with him, he confirmed we should not go anywhere we weren't impressed, told us there was hope at Duke, that I needed radiation, and that Duke would take amazing care of me if we came down.

I said it before, and I'll say it again, hope is a powerful thing.

We decided we'd need to plan a little trip down to Duke. At four hours away from home, Duke wasn't somewhere I could commute for care, so if we decided to have radiation there, we'd need to stay in Durham, North Carolina. We decided we'd figure that part out when we got to it. When we arrived at Duke, we were taken into a conference room and a parade of people came through, including Dr. Friedman. What's amazing about Duke in comparison to other places I have been both before and since is they really get how incredibly awful it is to have a brain tumor, and because of that, they have developed an approach that revolves around the patient. Over the next hour or so, we met my oncology nurse, the brain tumor center pharmacist, a social worker for me, a social worker for my children, my radiation oncology nurse, and my radiation oncologist. We were also given information on support groups for patients, care givers, families, and information on where we could stay near Duke so I could get treatment. My brain had cancer, but we all needed care and treatment, and they really got that.

After talking to my radiation oncologist, Dr. John Kirkpatrick, we knew we needed to be at Duke. In addition to surrounding my entire family with the support that we needed, Dr. Kirkpatrick was fully awesome, too. I mean the man had radiation symbol cufflinks. Dr. Kirkpatrick felt confident about his plan to use the Novalis system ("millimeter accuracy!") to treat my brain stem, not my whole brain or spine, but he talked us through his thought process and included us. This was our doctor.

We visited Caring House, which is like a Ronald McDonald House for adults being treated at Duke. People are allowed to stay there for a very low rate, making the stay for treatment economically feasible. Caring House does absolutely amazing work, but I called it "Casa Di Cancer" because I felt like I would drown in encouraging activities. There were support groups, crafting your feelings, and a totally cancer-steeped environment, which I didn't think I could handle. Also, my kids weren't allowed to come there when they visited. We ended up deciding on a hotel with long-term medical rates, and we went home to figure the rest out.

And Then We Blasted
That Mother....

Before I started treatment, I had another appointment at Duke for some preliminary testing. First, I had to get another MRI, and then I had to get fitted for a radiation mask. For other parts of your body, radiation involves getting small tattoos that show where the beams should go in. Thankfully, for my type, they don't tat up your face and claim it will give you street cred. But more on that later.

My MRI took forever (you may be sensing a theme here). They had to keep switching the headpieces and they did it with and without contrast. By the end of the MRI, my head was starting to really hurt from laying on my incision, which just so happens to be on the exact location where all of the weight from my head ends up. When I sat up, it went away, so I thought I was okay. When they put me in the CT machine to do the mask, though, the pain came back and became unbearable around twenty minutes into the mask hardening.

Luckily, Austin had come back to sit with me, so he called the nurse to ask her how much longer. She said thirty more minutes, and asked if I'd like a little something for the pain. Austin laughed until I said, "Yes, right now," and he proceeded to explain that I try to avoid pain medication like the plague, so if I'm asking for it without being offered, it must be bad. Unfortunately, they gave me something that didn't work, and I think the pain was compounded by my brain having this conversation:

Pain Center: "SIT UP YOU GIANT IDIOT! THIS HURTS!"
Logical Center: "Oh, hello, friend. We're kind of strapped in here."
Pain Center: "I WILL CUT YOU!"
Logical Center: "If we make them get us out, we'll just have to start again."
Pain Center: "SIT UP! SIT UP! SIT UP!"
Logical Center: "Actually, this rather hurts. Maybe you should sit up. Oh, goodness, we're trapped."
Pain Center: "WE'RE ALL GONNA DIEEEEE!"
Logical Center: "TRUTH! WE'RE ALL GONNA DIEEEEE!"

How the mask process works is they put some plastic wrap on your head and lay you down in warm goop. Then, they put a bite plate in your mouth and put warm plastic pieces over your chin and forehead. Next, they put warm plastic mesh over all that. When it's molded to their satisfaction, they cover you up with cold washcloths to help cool the plastic, and then you lay still for forty to fifty minutes until the mask is hard.

Once you have your mask, you start daily radiation. Treatment only takes about ten minutes. That meant I spent most of my time sitting in our room while Austin telecommuted. I read, I watched TV,

I napped, and I eavesdropped on his work meetings because I was bored. Well, that's not entirely true. Initially we were in the most awful hotel on earth. Perfect, because brain cancer really needs an extra side of awful. The sheets had cigarette burns, the room was non-smoking, but sucked in smoke from an attached room on the opposite side of the hotel whenever they turned their bathroom fan on, and we could barely stand to be in the room with the door closed. We tried air fresheners, charcoal bags, and everything that we could possibly come up with. It was actually really depressing to come "home" to that, and one day I just stayed in the car reading on my iPhone. The week our kids came down to visit and stayed at a La Quinta nearby, Austin just switched us. This presented a new problem, however, because initially he couldn't get good enough internet at the new hotel to telecommute, so I got really good at sleeping in the Duke "Cancer Palace" cafeteria, in the comfy chairs in the lab waiting room, and even on the outdoor benches in the courtyard. I was so thankful he could work and be there with me, I didn't really mind. Once his boss found out, though, he overnighted Austin a hotspot to use in our hotel.

When Austin finished work, he tried to keep my spirits up and keep me active, even as I got progressively more tired. We went on walks and out for ice cream and it was manageable. Backing up a little, my first day of radiation was horrible. I came back, felt nauseous, had a headache, and felt disoriented. I was upset because I heard radiation wasn't going to be bad at first, but after a long nap, I felt better on day two. After that, radiation wasn't much to comment on for a few weeks. Occasionally I would get these horrendous metallic-tasting burps, which is the most random complaint in the world. If you ever have radiation and you get them, too, the good news is you can make them go away by eating Sweet Frog Frozen Yogurt. You can substitute Ben and Jerry's in a pinch, but I preferred Sweet Frog, so I could get gummy bears. Frozen gummy bears are a thing of beauty. Luckily, eating wasn't something I was interested in since the surgery, so I didn't get any fatter from my ice cream consumption during radiation.

We went home on weekends to see the kids and go to their sporting events. On week three, they came down with my momma and spent the week with me, and it was the happiest week I had. It was nice to have distractions and to be able to leave the room and go out. I'm not complaining. Austin's incredible employer let him telecommute, and I know he had to get stuff done. I wouldn't have gone anywhere, anyway, but having mom and the kids around was great. I rallied all of the energy I had that week and we enjoyed excursions around Durham as much as I could stand, although they mostly involved sitting. We took the kids to a children's museum where I sat and watched them, to a Durham Bulls game—I sat in the stands and at some point dozed off on my mom's shoulder—and to a movie. Nothing was very taxing on my energy levels. I think the most we did were some walks in a local park, but I was so happy to be with them, and I wanted to do as much as I could, so they'd remember having fun with me.

By the end of week 4, I got tired. At first it was just a little more tired, but then it was TIRED. Tired like "chewing sounds like effort" and tired like "should I get up and go to the bathroom, or should we tip the maid more because the bathroom is like, five feet away." Helpful hint for those of you supporting someone receiving brain radiation: They're getting worse every day, not better. So when you are trying to encourage them, go with, "You're getting closer to being done!" and not, "This is making you better!" or, "You're getting stronger every day!" because they're actually getting weaker and worse every day.

Some people don't have side effects from radiation—I feel like I should mention that. But for those that do, exhaustion is one of the most common side effects. Also, your brain is probably going to swell a little bit, so any neurological symptoms you had will get worse. My left side neuropathy got much worse than it was when I finished PT with my brother, which was because of the swelling happening as a response to the radiation. Typically, they can give you steroids to help combat that, and it helps with the tiredness, too, but since I was a super genius and got bronchitis during my final weeks of treatment, they didn't want to give me steroids because they repress your immune system and getting pneumonia wasn't something any of us were interested in.

Did I remind you guys to ask before touching someone who's getting any kind of brain treatments? You should. Frequently the side effects make no sense, and you can't see them. The invisible man stabbing my leg, for example, doesn't really make sense to anyone because nobody did anything to my legs, but when someone pats my leg because I'm sitting down, and they want to be kind, it hurts like the devil! Same with rubbing my arm, bumping into me, or patting my shoulder on the left side. All reasons I avoided crowded situations, or strategically put Austin or my mother to the left of me.

My only other big side effect happened at the intersection of weeks 4 and 5 when my hair started falling out in the radiation pattern. It drove me nuts because I'd grown back about an inch of hair, which was just enough to fall down my shirt or stick on me in the shower. Luckily, the clippers and I fixed that. I had cute hats—I didn't need hair. Also, I had hoop earrings and scarves. That whole "look in the mirror and remove one accessory" thing doesn't count when you're bald. You can have as many pieces of flair as you want.

Note: People with claustrophobia, brain tumors are not for you. In addition to all the MRIs in a tube, you get to wear the aforementioned mask every stinkin' day for treatment. I found it best to not think about it. I closed my eyes every day before they put it on and tried to zone out to somewhere else. I don't have claustrophobia, but if I thought about how I was now basically Leonardo Di Caprio in *The Man in the Iron Mask*, I would really start to freak out. There was a little girl who went before me, and she frequently pitched a fit about getting put into her mask. I can't say I blame her because I wanted to do the same thing. I think nine-tenths of "adulting" is telling your inner 2-year-old that it can't have its way, and that you're not going to think about it anymore.

There were a lot of things I chose not to think about.

I chose not to think about the fact that I was strapped down to a table by my face while people shot beams of radiation at my brain. I chose not to think about the possibility of Posterior Fossa Syndrome, which is basically when they mess with your brain stem so much that you turn into a vegetable for a few weeks. I chose not to think about the fact that we were buying time because everyone was telling me this thing was going to come back and they were just promising me they were buying time to have better treatment options by then. Much like the mask, I choose not to think about it. Much like my surgery, worrying about it won't change the outcome. We did everything we could do, and it all went as well as it could—and the rest we left to God.

That Time My Husband Brought a Wheelchair, or, Things I Bet Divorce Lawyers Haven't Heard Before

The Race for Hope, a 5K that raises funds for brain cancer research, had been on my radar since before my surgery. I signed my whole family up to participate before the scalpel touched my head, and it was the goal that kept me pushing through physical therapy. I know people joke all the time that when there's a problem in America, we try to solve it with a 5K, but in this case, it really did help me to have a goal to work toward. My goal was to walk the three miles, not to run or set a personal record, and I think if we'd had the race before radiation, I would have been fine.

But, as luck would have it, it was after week 5.

By week 5 of radiation, I slept most of the day, shuffled instead of walking because I was too tired to pick my feet up, and lived off of two to three bites a day of frozen yogurt. Austin switched from calling me his

59

hummingbird to calling me Quasimodo. I thought I looked more like a velociraptor, but he wasn't wrong, either.

The Race for Hope was in downtown D.C., and we had to leave fairly early in the morning, which was fine since I just slept in the car. My mom had packed my grandmother's wheelchair for me, so after we parked in the garage, Austin wanted to bring it "just in case" I got too tired to finish the race.

I would love to tell you I appreciated how thoughtful and supportive my husband was trying to be. I would love to tell you I found beauty in the fact that he was going to walk beside me as far as I could go, and if I didn't have the strength to finish, he was going to push me the rest of the way. But you've been reading for a while now, so I feel like you already know that didn't happen.

I rallied what little energy I had to have an absolute temper tantrum. How could they have betrayed me by even bringing the wheelchair? Why did no one believe I was strong? How did they expect me to fight this disease if they didn't even think I could walk? I stormed out of the parking garage promising I wouldn't speak to anyone ever again if that wheelchair left the trunk of my van.

The Race for Hope was about a block-and-a-half from where we parked, and I realized I was a giant idiot for leaving the wheelchair in the car approximately four feet outside of the parking garage. But, dedicated as always to my poor decision making, I soldiered on.

Once we reached staging, there was a survivors' tent where Austin accompanied me and where we met David Cook from American Idol—a huge supporter of the race who lost his brother to brain cancer while he was on the show. There were lots of survivors in yellow shirts like mine, many of them using wheelchairs or walkers, which my husband was brilliant to keep to himself and not make a point of highlighting for me. David Cook led a survivors' walk to start the race, which I chose not to participate in. In fact, in the years since, I still haven't participated in the survivors' walk, but that's a totally different subject.

I don't remember for sure, but I believe it took me—and my very patient family and friends—two hours to do the Quasimodo shuffle for 3.1 miles. In case you're trying to do the math, that's approximately a 25-minute mile. I have a few friends who could have run the entire race nine times in the time it took me to cross the finish line.

I took a nap in the car and was in pain for the rest of the week. Good choices. It's a theme.

I guess that's the takeaway: there is no shame in taking a little bit of help. It doesn't matter if you cross the finish line on your own two feet, or in a wheelchair, because you're still crossing the finish line.

But that would be a lie. The real point is I finished all by myself. I win. Hahaha.

And Now, We Wait.

After finishing up radiation, there was little to do except wait for the ependymoma to come back, or not. The excruciating part of having brain cancer is that every time you forget a word, every time your head hurts, every time you stumble, you wonder if "it" is back.

And you really have no way to know.

Recovery was hard. I was so tired, and I beat myself up frequently because I felt like I should be better. People around me were celebrating that I was "done," and I had "beaten" the ependymoma, but I was exhausted, and I knew that it could come back. One day, my family finally left me for the day with the promise I would eat something while they were gone. I think they went out on the boat with the kids. At noon, I walked down the stairs to the kitchen, at which point, I had to sit down and rest. I took something out of the fridge to warm up in the microwave, and after putting it in, I had to sit down and rest. By the time I got the food from the microwave to the table, I ended up falling asleep next to my plate. I woke up an hour later sorry that I'd slept with my head in that position, but thankful I didn't have hair since it would have been covered in whatever I was supposed to be eating.

As I was healing, I also had a lot of trouble dealing with survivor's guilt. The more I learned about other types of gliomas, the luckier I believed I should feel. I struggled with being a "survivor" because I didn't feel like I earned that title, and I knew in the back of my mind I wasn't completely done. I wrote this on my family blog summarizing how I felt about the whole survivor concept:

I'm Not a Survivor

Austin approached me last night and told me he felt like I paint an overly rosy picture of my diagnosis. "You make it sound like you have a sinus infection," he claimed. "Don't make it the end of the world but be honest about it."

Here's the thing. I have mixed feelings about that. Is an ependymoma fantastic? No, it's not. If you get to pick your brain tumor, you should pick a benign meningioma right under your skull. They pop them out like pimples or leave them in depending on size. They don't hurt anything, and frequently they only find them by accident. Ependymomas are rare, and they're in a terrible location. Most adults get them in their spine, which is a horrible place to need surgery. I got mine around my brain stem, which is dangerous. We didn't leave our kids for six weeks to get radiation treatment because the Cancer Center is pretty. We left because it's a complex region to treat and we needed good, experienced doctors. Do you know what posterior fossa syndrome is? It's where your brain shuts off. It happens in people who've had surgery or radiation to the back of their brain, where I did. They don't know why it happens, it just does.

However, I have a strange approach to this whole thing. Half the reason I shaved my head before surgery was because I wasn't letting my brain tumor take anything away from me. It couldn't take my hair because I gave it up. I needed doctors who, even if they acknowledged it was the wrong choice, told me I had a choice because my brain tumor wasn't allowed to force me into doing something I didn't want to do, like brain surgery. I needed to pick it because I wanted to, and I had choices.

I don't want to be my brain tumor. I don't want people telling me I'm "amazing" or "strong," and I don't want to be a survivor. Partially because this is something that happened and not my identity, and partially because it seems wrong and unfair. Also, partially because nobody wants to do this, you just have to do it. I don't feel amazing or strong. I don't feel like I'm "an inspiration." I just feel like I was sick and couldn't take care of my family the way I wanted, and that sucks.

Doing the Race for Hope almost gave me a panic attack because of that stupid yellow shirt. I feel like what I've been through is not legitimate compared to others. This lady, Carol, has an ependymoma, and she has struggled to maintain the ability to walk, talk, and do other basic functions because of the damage to her brain. Some people lose their children, their sweet precious babies to this thing. Mark has had three surgeries, chemo and radiation to try to kill off his ependymoma.

It seems like I got it pretty easy with minimal side effects and a successful surgery.

Beyond that, as one person mentioned to me online, "Ependymomas barely count;" not because the process isn't hard or scary, or because the location isn't ideal (it isn't) but because when you consider the fact that survival in adults is so high, and then you look at something like Glioblastoma Multiforme, which kills almost universally, it does seem like I had a sinus infection—a really bad one, but still, it could be so much worse.

It's a hard balance that I am trying to strike. I don't want to be defined by this forever. I don't want a vanity plate with a grey ribbon. I don't want to become a walking awareness PSA. I don't want to be told, "You're just such a fighter" as if the people who don't make it to the other side of their brain tumor didn't try hard enough. I want to help raise money for a cure because I don't want anyone to ever have to do this, but I don't want to walk (and didn't) as a survivor because I feel like I'm somehow faking it because it could've been so much worse for me than it was.

So, in conclusion, I apologize if you felt slighted that you brought my family food and all I had was a sinus infection. It is definitely more than that, but at the same time, I got it pretty easy when you consider how successful my surgery was, how long I made it on radiation with no symptoms, and the fact that they removed my entire tumor. I had it pretty easy. Or, as easy as you can have it with sixteen hours of surgery and six weeks of radiation. I guess being thankful for that makes me tend to gloss over the severity of my situation, but I'd rather that than be a puddle on the floor.

Sometimes, You Get a Little Postpartum Depression

Recovery is a tough thing for many reasons. There's the physical symptoms, the exhaustion, the uncertainty, but there's also a lot of mental "stuff" that goes on. When I look back at the things I wrote during my recovery period, I realized I suffered from some serious postpartum depression after "birthing" my ependymoma from my brain.

Yes, I called it postpartum depression. Here's why. I took a list of postpartum depression symptoms and changed it from "motherhood" to "recovery."

1. You have feelings of being overwhelmed. Not like "this is hard," but like "I can't do this, and I'm never going to be able to do this."

2. You feel guilty because you feel like you should be handling recovery better than this.

3. You feel guilty because you're not blissful that you survived and the people around you are. You feel angry/hurt/tired and guilty about having those feelings.
4. You feel irritated or angry. Everything annoys you.
5. You feel nothing. You feel empty and devoid of emotion.
6. You can't bring yourself to eat.
7. You feel disconnected and like you are separated from the rest of the world.
8. You're afraid you lost the "old you" and you will be stuck feeling like this for the rest of your life.

So, yeah, postpartum depression from your tumor. It sucks. It's made worse by several things.

First, it's made worse by the sudden alienation. People who were incredibly present and supportive when I was diagnosed, and whom I didn't know were my friends, vanished as suddenly as they jumped into my life when I finished treatment. I am still grateful for everything they did for me, but being suddenly abandoned by people leaves you with a sense that you were just a project, and now you're worthless to a group of people who were only interested in helping you because you were sick. That's a really strange thing.

Second, survivor's guilt is very real. I think for many of the people I've talked to about it, you can find a way to have it no matter what. You can feel guilty because you survived breast cancer and someone else's mom did not. You can feel guilty every time someone posts a memorial on Facebook about the friend they lost to cancer, even if it's not the type you had, just because you feel badly they're missing someone and you still get to be here. You can feel guilty that you got "the easy kind" of cancer like I mentioned feeling. I didn't get a glioblastoma, so I should feel lucky.

Listen, it's all total garbage. There is no "Oh, I got grade 1 breast cancer! #blessed!" Certainly, you can be excited you had good news, but there is no good cancer, and there is no reason for you to feel badly that someone else didn't make it. You are here for a purpose, whatever that is, and you did not inject that other person with the cancer that took their life, so it's not your fault they died.

Stemming from survivor's guilt is the idea that you're still here and just totally wasting everyone else's time and energy—that you shouldn't still get to be here because what you're doing is not worth what you went through. Here's something I wrote in my journal back in June of 2013.

On Worth

Getting better is hard for me, not because of the physical, but because of the mental. I am a huge "man up" fan, so dealing with the pain, while not fun, has been okay. What really bothers me is not being "back to normal" already. You know, because it's June and I had sixteen hours of brain surgery in February, so really, what gives? I know that in the grand scheme of things I am doing way better than we ever could have hoped, but I'm not "back." I want to be driving and taking care of my kids and my house and back to being myself. I'm running my website again, which is nice, but based solely on the fact that my website can be done ahead in chunks when I feel good. I pre-post things to Facebook/Twitter/Blogger and then it looks like I'm always doing well :) It's a good trick!

Today, the kids went to camp. Riley and Logan are doing Cub Scout Camp, which my mom is attending every day. I know that she loves the kids and she wouldn't do things if she didn't want to, but the fact she's out there getting bitten up and sunburned instead of me gives me guilt. Savannah Lynn is doing a skating camp, which I'm sure she'll love, but I've never sent my kids away for a week at such a young age, and I know the party line around here (because my mom and Austin love me) was "It wouldn't be fair" for Savannah not to get to do something fun, and not "you're incapable of being fun all day alone," but I know that she's really at camp because I'm not back to being a good enough mom.

It took me a really long time to feel like I was doing anything worthwhile with my life to begin with. I'd always gone along with the "career first, family later" mentality and really got sucked into "you can be anything you want" idea, but that never included being a mom. I tied my entire identity into grades and awards and my ability to "be" things. I wanted to have a job title that made me important, so when I had Riley, I struggled to not suck at being a mom and to still be "someone." I'm not sure how many student government senators have kids, for example, but I had to keep doing it. I didn't even tell my professors I was pregnant with Logan until I was two weeks from my due date, and then only because one of them asked. When I finished school and started staying home full-time, I really struggled, too, because I wasn't "doing anything." I still felt like I had to prove myself and host more playdates, make sure that Riley and Logan were better at things; push, push, push. It wasn't really until after I had Savannah that I had any kind of peace about who I was.

I spent a lot of time in scripture after Savannah. I prayed on the idea that my role could be helping Austin and raising our children and that those things weren't just sufficient, they were an entire calling. It was a totally new perspective for me that washing laundry, feeding my family and loving my kids, when done for a purpose of pleasing God, was enough. I was enough. I didn't have to justify myself to anyone; I didn't have to fight to be important. In fact, my marriage got markedly better when I stopped fighting Austin for control. Shocker. Anyway, that means it took me five years to get myself together and figure out that being a wife and a mom was worthwhile and I could pour myself into that and rest knowing that I wasn't just leaching oxygen from the senators, lawyers, and CEOs out there.

Now, because I can't even do that, I'm struggling again. Today, I made pretzels. The kids were at camp, I felt pretty good, I decided to make pretzels. It took me a long time because I'm still slower than normal—although nowhere near as bad as I was—and by the time I was done and cleaned up I was exhausted.

Today, all I did was make pretzels.

Is that worth anything? Do my doctors ever go home at night and think about what a waste of effort I must seem? Hundreds of thousands of dollars have gone into my care, and countless man-hours in medical staff planning, operating and implementing, and following up. So much work and effort and money…

And today, I was exhausted by pretzels.

If you're still here, the work was worth it. Every hug, every kiss, yes, even every pretzel is worth you being here—the work was done to save you. Every survivor helps heal the next person with your diagnosis; every struggle helps the doctors do better next time; and all the pain and heartache you are going through with your family as you suffer and recover are making you stronger, better, more compassionate people.

Keep Going.

Also, don't be afraid to join a support group or to ask for anti-depressants. I know a lot of people look down on needing a little better living through chemistry, but if you're in a tough place during treatment or recovery, remember so much has been done to your body, and just like you wouldn't deny yourself insulin if your body didn't produce it, you shouldn't deny yourself a little help producing serotonin when your body has forgotten how to be happy. You are no less awesome and no less of an overcomer if you take a hand up from the ground that you find yourself on.

And Slowly, You Start Feeling Almost Normal Again....

I t took me a really long time to feel normal. Not "new normal," although it might be that's what I am, but I rejected settling for a new normal and pushed myself to feel like I was back to who I was before. We've already established that I make really poor decisions about being kind to myself where my own expectations are concerned.

Small victories add up: you'll stay up a few hours at a time; you'll make dinner all by yourself; you'll work a full day; you'll drive the car; and suddenly, one day, you'll be able to make it through a day without thinking about what happened to you—about how you've changed inherently due to what has happened. Before you realize it, you are just living your life.

Unfortunately, with cancer, there are constant reminders that you're not okay. You'll be living your life and then you have to go to the oncologist for a checkup. You'll be living your life and have your breath taken away because you need an MRI and scanxiety is a real thing. Even if you are normally a calm person, thinking about the potential results can mess up the entire week before your scan. Laying in the MRI machine, CT scan, or PET scan can be harder than ever because you are so worried. Instead of lying there motionless, you want to scream at the tech to tell you what's going on. After the scans are done, waiting for the results is like waiting for Santa to come, but not in a fun way.

Cancer is like an annoying neighbor that goes on vacation for weeks at a time and suddenly pops back in and rings the doorbell to borrow something. Just when you thought they were gone for good, they're back wanting to ruin something else of yours. Even if your scans stay clean, that fear is there in the back of your mind just waiting.

I finally got back to normal. It took a long time, and many really interesting haircuts, but I did it. True story, the natural style of my hair is mullet. Business in the front, party in the back all the way. I rocked that sucker for weeks waiting for my hair to grow long enough to actually have a real style that didn't make me look like Joe Dirt. You don't know me, so I'll explain some of what normal means for me.

I am a mother of three kids and wife to an awesome husband. He works full-time, and I homeschool our three children and run them around to an insane number of activities. I teach classes in a few homeschool co-ops, in addition to teaching my children what they need to know at home. I volunteer in my church and community. In my spare time, I own a business called Prince William County Moms, worked for our state delegate, and volunteer. Normal takes a lot of energy and effort. Lest you think this is me bragging about how awesome I am, I actually think it's a testimony to me being clinically insane and doing too much.

When I'm not doing all of those things, I try to read and run. I do the reading better than the running. To quote my favorite t-shirt, "I run slower than a turtle going uphill in molasses, but I run." The only definite on my calendar each year is the Race for Hope on the first Sunday in May, but it was because of that race I changed my feelings about "being" my diagnosis.

Silver Sparkles

In case you missed the part about me being a magical unicorn, let me take this opportunity to remind you that my friends decided that was my spirit animal. It only makes sense that plain, grey brain tumor awareness ribbons weren't going to suffice for my crew and me. As I approached my one year "survive-a-versary," I decided I wanted to commemorate my survival and my 30th birthday in a big way, so I came up with the idea of doing "30 for 30," a challenge where I would do 30 Acts of Kindness in celebration of my 30th birthday, culminating in a fundraiser for the Race for Hope.

I created my list by asking my readers on Prince William County Moms, my business, what I should do. They gave me a pretty extensive list, with lots of varied ideas, and I enjoyed each one of them. I wrote about the project, too, hoping that people would find a way to volunteer in the community, even if they had small kids and couldn't do something huge or time consuming. We filled up gumball machines at the grocery store with quarters, paid for the order of the people in front of us, handed out flowers to the crossing guards, served dinners at the homeless shelter, served "Soup and Socks" with a local group called The 25th Project, took cookies to firefighters, and more. We had a great time, and it was an amazing way for me to really feel like there was purpose in still being alive. Even if you are still feeling awful during recovery, doing tiny acts of kindness, like filling the vending machine, can make you feel fantastic. It's such a small thing, but if you happen to catch the smile on the face of the person getting a free soda or bouncy ball, it's totally worth it.

The fundraiser for the Race for Hope was the hardest of the tasks to complete because it required so much planning—not my forte—and because it involved me recanting my position that I wasn't going to "be" my illness. I didn't want to turn into one of "those" people who talked about their cancer all the time and owned every pink ribbon thing ever produced. While the second part was easy—almost no one makes grey ribbon products, so the temptation to buy every brain cancer awareness item you ever see at a store will not send you to the poor house—the first part turned out to be even easier. There's a scene in the movie *Mean Girls* where Lindsay Lohan's character says she was constantly looking for a reason to talk about her arch-nemesis, and when she couldn't bring her up, she was hoping other people would bring her up so she could talk about her. Then the words came out like word vomit; she almost couldn't help it.

That's kind of me with my brain cancer. And I'm not so sure that's a bad thing.

First of all, talking about my surgery, my treatment, and my recovery helped give others hope. Whether it was the people around me, or friends of friends who were diagnosed and given my phone number as someone to contact, I'm grateful that as a side effect of my cancer, I have been able to be there for other people facing something similar. Second, talking about what happened to me was cathartic. I felt better talking about it. Third, watching the faces people make when you tell them you had brain cancer is kind of fun. They're never quite sure what to do. It's kind of fun to watch in a twisted sort of way.

Silver Sparkles Family Fun Day ended up being a big success. I'd never hosted an event of that size before, and I learned a lot. At the end of the day, it was worth all the hard work talking about my cancer on TV to drum up interest, and the shameless pulling of every favor I'd ever been offered. At the time of writing, we're now in our sixth year and have been able to donate tens of thousands of dollars to brain cancer research. For me, that's important because as I mentioned before, ependymomas don't typically respond well to chemotherapy and with a limited number of drugs that even cross the blood-brain barrier, I look at it as literally raising money to save my own life.

Another reason research funding is important is because brain cancer research is grossly underfunded considering its death rate. In fiscal year 2015, the National Cancer Institute reported they would spend $543,700,000 on breast cancer, compared with $202,100,000 on brain cancer. I'm not picking on breast cancer, it's just one example[1]. The five-year relative survival rate for breast cancer varies by stage at diagnosis, but the overall five-year survival rate is 90%, whereas the five-year overall survival rate for brain cancer is 34%[2]. There aren't currently five-year survival statistics for Glioblastoma Multiforme because there aren't enough survivors at that point to be statistically significant. Money, drugs, and research for brain cancer need to happen faster, and I am happy to do what I can to be a part of that process.

---

1   National Institutes of Health (NIH), "Funding for Research Areas," NIH National Cancer Institute, last modified December 20, 2018, accessed February 21, 2019, https://www.cancer.gov/about-nci/budget/fact-book/data/research-funding.

2   American Society of Clinical Oncology, "What is Survivorship?," Cancer.net, last modified May 2018, accessed February 21, 2019, https://www.cancer.net/survivorship/what-survivorship.

If you'd like to become more involved with raising money for brain tumor and brain cancer research, you can check out braintumor.org and look for events in your local area.

Not Necessarily Correlated

As time went on, it got easier to forget between scans that I was still at risk. I was so busy with work, kids, homeschool, and family that I was able to put my illness mostly out of my mind. There were certainly frustrations, for example, brain and spine MRIs are the standard of care for ependymoma patients since they frequently "drop" metastes into the spine from the brain, but my insurance decided I no longer needed spinal MRIs my second year of recovery. My oncologist fought them tooth and nail but decided we could take a few years off since I was asymptomatic, and we could fight for them at regular intervals, just not as frequently as the brain scans.

During my year of recovery, right in the middle of my first Silver Sparkles event, my husband and I moved our family out of our townhouse and into a single-family home about thirty minutes away from where we'd been living. It was a fixer-upper with beautiful bones and a creek in the backyard.

We are truly gluttons for punishment.

When we moved, I found a great group of friends through an organization called Moms Run This Town/She Runs This Town, which is a national running group for women. I started running with a core group of people and soon they convinced me to sign up for my first half-marathon.

Yes, I am telling you I ran a half marathon, just like I told you that I ran the 10-miler. Again, my memoir, my rules, and I want it in writing that I was able to run 13.1 miles at some point in my life. Now, the fact that I did medium-sized runs and (spoiler alert: diagnosis two is coming) was diagnosed with brain cancer is not necessarily correlated. No one actually knows what causes people to have brain tumors. There are some incidentals out there. Al Musella, who runs Virtual Trials, has collected tons and tons of information on patients over the years, and while his online community isn't scientific, they've definitely noticed patterns even doctors have yet to confirm. I claim my brain tumor is caused by a chronic allergy to stupid. I think the 2016 presidential debates pushed me over the edge. I shouldn't have watched them.

Anyway, a few months after my half marathon, I started having a lot of lower back pain when I ran and when I drove long distances. My half was in October, and starting in January, my oldest son was part of the Page Program at the Virginia House of Delegates. He had to be driven to Richmond every Sunday and picked up from Richmond every Friday. That's a three-plus hour round trip drive depending on traffic. As time went on, it became harder and harder to be comfortable during the drive. I started doing all kinds of quasi-legal things, like driving with my left foot propped up on the dash board, sitting on my left foot part of the drive, and generally assuming any position I could to take the pain off of my back.

I saw my general practitioner who told me to give it a few weeks and then follow up with a spine center if it didn't get better. I visited the spine center at the end of January and they scheduled an MRI to make sure I didn't have a slipped disc or hernia of any kind. The MRI was supposed to be on February 6, which is a good day for me. February 6 is the day I celebrate my survive-a-versary. Unfortunately, when I arrived for my scan, there was an issue with the paperwork. They bumped me while they got it taken care of. I watched people go back and come out and every time they left, the tech who walked them to the door would say, "Have a great day, your doctor will have the results in two to three days."

When I was finally taken back for my scan, everything went as it normally does. I laid in the tiny plastic coffin, quizzed myself on times tables, and then changed back into my clothes. The tech walked me out and said, "Your doctor will receive your results."

I stopped dead in my tracks and looked at her. "Excuse me?" I questioned. She repeated herself verbatim. I walked like a zombie to my car and called my husband. I told him it was probably nothing, but I was completely freaked out by the fact that she didn't say to me what she'd said to everyone else. He assured me if we made it to the end of the day with no phone call everything was fine. The end of the day came and went with no phone call, so we were in the clear.

The next day was Tuesday, which was our homeschool co-op day. During my moms' group meeting at the beginning of the day, I had a tiny freak out moment as we were praying for another mom who'd just found out she had breast cancer. When we went over to pray for her, my friend Tammy put her hand right on my lower back where the pain was, and as she did, my phone rang. Luckily, it was on vibrate, because if you go to church you know that if you interrupt intercessory prayer time with your ring tone, it better be Jesus calling. It wasn't Jesus, but it was the spine center, which I saw after we finished praying. My heart leapt into my throat, and I ran into the hallway to call back.

No worries. They were just calling to remind me that my appointment was on Wednesday.

I spent the rest of the day laughing at myself. I was worried about nothing. They weren't calling to tell me anything was wrong, I still had my pre-planned appointment and everything was okay. Hey, I even got the spine MRI my insurance had refused the last few years! This was a bonus. My oncologist would be so proud of me!

On Wednesday, my day was pretty standard: my oldest son called me in the morning as he walked to work at the state capital; I did school with my younger children; I answered a bunch of emails; and then I headed out for my appointment. I left my middle son in charge of my daughter. He was old enough to be left home during the day for an hour, and I headed to my appointment about 8 minutes from the house. When the physician's assistant I saw the first time took me back, he asked if my pain had changed at all. I told him it hadn't. He said unfortunately what they were seeing on my MRI was what looked like drop metastases from my previous cancer.

I stayed pretty calm, and why not, I already knew in the back of my mind what was going on. I asked to see the MRI and the physician's assistant took me back to the workroom to show me what he was seeing. There it was right on the screen. The blobs showing me that the ependymoma I had "beaten" had just been playing a game of hide-and-seek.

When I went back to the room, the PA asked me to stay put until the doctor, who I'd never met, could talk to me. I snuck in a call to my friend Stacey and asked her to get my kids. I knew the bus was coming to drop her children off, and I promised I wouldn't ask if it wasn't an emergency. She asked me if my cancer was back. When I couldn't answer her, she just said, "Don't you worry, girl, we got this, and I've got your babies. I promise they will be fine." I called my husband at work, and caught him at a bad time. He told me he couldn't really talk. I think was a little frustrated when I didn't say anything for a minute, but there was a giant bubble in my throat from where I was trying to swallow my tears. When I finally croaked something out to him, all I could say was, "It's back," and then I cried. He asked where I was and told me he was leaving right then.

I don't remember much of what the spine doctor said. It was strange to have a doctor I had never met trying to temper the news that my cancer was back in my spine. I know the things I said to him were not what I was thinking. I remember apologizing for crying and for agreeing that people live with this but actually thinking, *"I know what this means. I know that recurrences are bad because chemo doesn't work. I know I was supposed to have more time."*

I sat in the front seat of my car and sobbed hysterically after leaving the spine center. I saw a sweet old couple heading in to the Dunkin Donuts on the bottom floor of the building to get some afternoon coffee, or maybe a donut (I don't know and I'm not here to judge). The woman stared back at me and ended up turning around and putting her hand on my driver's side window. She didn't say anything; just stood there and gave me a sad smile. It was the most oddly comforting thing to know that at that moment I wasn't alone. She probably thought I was crazy and having some kind of crisis over falling off my diet plan, but her taking a moment to comfort me, even in that disconnected way, helped me calm down enough to drive to the hospital to get a disc of my MRI for my oncologist at Georgetown and to send to my radiation oncologist at Duke, and then go home.

When I got home, I didn't have to wait long for Austin to get there and envelop me in a hug. With my first diagnosis, I went quickly to a place of faith and peace. With this diagnosis, I went to fear and depression.

Really Quickly.

A Love Note to
My Insurance Company

It has been my experience that the purpose of health insurance is to promote the Darwinian evolution of our population by ensuring that only the most obnoxious and fastidious survive. It's not been our experience that since we have great health insurance things just happen like they should, get paid for, and we're good to go. Before we transition into the more faith-filled part of this journey, I want to make sure you know how good and wretched I am by presenting you with this letter I've never actually sent to my insurance provider.

Dear My Insurance,

I know that as a company, it is your job to make money. I also know that we pay you every month, and four of the people in my household only get yearly physicals and the occasional antibiotics for an ear infection. According to the National Brain Tumor Society, brain tumors have the highest per-patient initial cost of care for any cancer group with an annualized mean cost of case in 2010 U.S. dollars of well over $100,000. That fact alone probably makes you happy that the survival rates are so low you don't have to keep paying out at that level over time, and I know that me still being here has messed with your bottom line.

I do appreciate how you work when you work. Receiving the bill for my craniotomy which, with the subsequent hospital stay, was almost $200,000 and seeing that the amount we owed was $0 made me understand salvation in a way I never had before because I'd never seen physical evidence of my outstanding debts being paid in full by someone else the way I did on that bill. Our townhouse cost $200,000, so seeing that my brain was the same price scared me to death. I'm also very thankful that instead of paying $130,000 for my year of temozolomide, I will only pay $360, which is $15 per bottle. I do think it's rather stupid that I have to pay two copayments because there aren't 105 milligram capsules, so I have to pay for a bottle of 100 milligram and a bottle of 5 milligram pills each month, whereas if I was on 100 or a higher 140, I'd only need to pay one copayment. But, that's more of a minor annoyance, like when hot dogs come in a 7-pack and buns come in an 8-pack. It bothers me, but in the grand scheme of things, I'm still saving $129,640, so thanks for that.

There are a lot of things I don't appreciate, though. First and foremost, I don't appreciate you deciding that you know better than my doctors what type of testing is medically necessary. My oncologist certainly did not go through all those years of medical school to argue with you that I needed spine MRIs, and you not letting me get them gave my ependymoma more time to grow than it should have had. I'm probably going to be ticked about that forever. I also don't love your customer service. When I was calling to try to fight with you about covering my monitoring MRIs, I actually had a customer service rep tell me that, "You've had a lot of MRIs, I feel like maybe you are just looking for more attention."

Say what?

That, unfortunately, did not get me on one of my better days, and after asking if she'd ever had an MRI, I may have suggested that she close herself in a coffin for two hours and let people make noises outside of it so she could understand that this was not an experience sought out like people showing up in the ER asking for opiates. Truly, you made the experience of trying to get the basic follow-up that every expert in neuro-oncology considers to be the standard of care impossible and frustrating in a way that, really, I feel you should receive some kind of award for.

Next, I don't appreciate when you just make things up. Remember that time after my laminectomy and six weeks of radiation and one cycle of chemotherapy when Duke called and said you were refusing to cover any of it because you decided that I had other insurance? That was fun. When my husband called you to deal with it, you told him you had decided that I'd been on his insurance for a long time, and so I'd probably gotten other insurance through my own employer, except I'm only part-time for the delegate I work for, and self-employed for my website, so there was no other insurance there. Then remember how you made us call Duke and have them re-submit every claim individually so you could pay what you owed? Even before that, I liked all the late charges I was getting from Georgetown because you were taking more than a month to pay them what you were supposed to. I just paid the fees because I didn't want to deal with you, but it didn't help you get off my "companies that suck" list.

Then there is the mail-order pharmacy. When Dante wrote his *Inferno,* I am confident he never had the experience of dealing with you—first of all because there were no phones and websites, but also because he would have included navigating insurance companies in his description of hell. I think my favorite part of that experience was getting a letter from you, after I'd already finished my first round of Temodar, that you were approving my need for the drug (thanks for that—since I'd already taken it), but that it all had to be ordered through your mail-order pharmacy. While we panicked a little that you might not have covered that first month, I went on to the website and set up an account linked to my healthcare ID. A few days later, we were going in circles trying to figure out why it wasn't showing up on my online chart as being ordered. I felt like I should have gotten a "bah dum ching" on drums like a bad joke at a comedy club when they told me they didn't have my insurance information. On your website.

Finishing up that fun experience involved an hour-and-a-half on the phone with not just the mail-order pharmacy, but the specialty mail order pharmacy—a totally separate company! After talking to the rep to get it ordered, I had to listen to a pharmacist tell me every possible side effect of a drug I'd already taken, including death. It's always fun to have that reminder. Thanks. Finally, when it came, I had to literally sit in my house all day waiting for UPS because my medication isn't supposed to be over 78 degrees or be stored in the bathroom because the moisture from the shower could potentially damage it, and I live in Virginia where the summer weather is mostly humid with a chance of hellfire. If the air isn't 104 degrees and so thick you could cut it with a knife, it's because it's raining, so you know, that's probably not ideal, either.

I know part of this is the delivery service's fault because even when I asked you to add delivery confirmation to my second order, the man in brown just chucked $17,000 of life-sustaining medication at my door and walked away. Luckily, I had anticipated this level of service when doing anything involving you guys and was sitting in my front room reading a book, so I got my medication right as it arrived rather than letting it sit on my doorstep in a thunderstorm.

In conclusion, thank you so much for all your help making sure that "survival of the most willing to keep fighting" continues to be a core value of your organization. I know that I'm definitely not the fittest, but your belief in my ability to keep giving up precious hours of my potentially limited life-span sitting on hold with you, or your subsidiaries and partners, has really helped raise my spirits by letting me know that you believe that even with brain cancer, I'm still mentally and physically able to pursue coverage of my necessary care like Liam Neeson hunting down the jerks who took his daughter. I hope that over the last four years you've realized that just like Liam, I, too, have a particular set of skills, and they involve being unaffected by listening to the same eight bars of music on hold for hours at a time, and a willingness to discuss my very private health concerns in the grocery store because I'm not going to sit at home on hold all day, so I take you with me and discuss it loud and proud wherever I am.

I look forward to continuing to work with you in the future to ensure I get the best possible care, not necessarily because you want to, but because I'm going to be a thorn in your side.

Love,

Kristina

Down the Rabbit Hole

There was absolutely no escaping the depression that surrounded me. As much as I tried to control my thoughts, I couldn't. I curled up into a ball on my bed and cried until my eyes could not cry anymore, and then I dry-sobbed. I did everything my doctors asked, and I did it with a smile. I did the surgery. I did the physical therapy. I did the daily radiation in a mask. I did the recovery. They told me I was buying more time—this was not the amount of time I was supposed to have purchased. I was supposed to be doing seven to ten years, which would have made my daughter 12 to 16, and she was only 8. My oncologist told me that in the time before my tumor came back, if it came back, she would find new protocols for me, and I knew there were not any breakthroughs in the four years I'd had. This stupid MRI even took my day away from me—February 6, my power day—and now it was the day my cancer came back.

While the first time around I didn't let the cancer take anything from me, this sneak attack took everything. It took my hope, it took my attitude, it took my ability to function, it even took my joy. In the midst of all that, I had to keep it together enough to not let my children know anything was wrong, especially since we didn't know how bad it was yet, and because Riley was living in Richmond until the end of February. I didn't want to rob him of the page experience.

We scheduled a visit with my oncologist and sent her the scans, which never arrived. When we met with her, I described what I'd seen, and she didn't seem very concerned. She wanted better MRIs and a brain scan, and for me to meet again with Dr. Nayar. I scheduled the MRIs, which unfortunately, had to be on different days. In the middle of all of this, I was planning Silver Sparkles 2017. It felt like I was drowning in brain cancer. When I wasn't worrying about my situation, I was advocating for my event and trying to smile. I stopped eating, barely slept, and by my event I was a mess. My brain MRI happened the Friday before my event. Lying to my children that I had a meeting for Silver Sparkles, I left them with Grammy, who again basically moved into our home to help take care of my children. The event fell on a Saturday, and I did a lot of sunglass wearing to cover my emotion. At my event, a very sweet woman whose mother was in the Duke Polio Study for Glioblastoma came. I noticed her "At Duke There is Hope" shirt, and she gave me a hug. I walked away and sobbed behind the building.

It was strange to have my event and not have everyone know what was going on. There were a few people who knew—my mother, husband and a few people from my Bible study class, none of whom had young children—so I was able to ask for them to pray for me knowing they wouldn't slip to my kids—and a few friends. Stacey obviously knew because she had to pick up my children the day I got the news. Lisa, my brain cancer go-to, knew because I called her immediately to cry, even though I already had doctors at Duke and wouldn't need her intervention, although I definitely needed her support. She came to the event to give me a kiss and tell me she "just didn't feel" the tumor was back in my brain. It was even harder to make it through the event because it's such an emotionally-charged day for so many of the people who come. People spent the day telling me how they came out because of someone they lost or someone that's fighting. They told me how they watched me go through the cancer the first time and be so brave, and I knew I was a puddle this time. It was really hard. At the end of the day, one of our vendors, Rob, who owns the "Stay Cheesy" food truck told me they just found out his stage 4 cancer was back. I cried and wrapped him in a hug, which was glorious because it was like hugging my brother. They're both tall, big guys, and tall, big guys give the best hugs. Rob told me to stop crying or he'd start. I told him I was so sorry, it was just that I'd just found out mine was back, too. Incidentally, at just that moment, the director of the hockey club my middle son plays in walked by, and taken aback, said, "Wait, whoa! Did I just hear what I thought I heard?" He took time to assure me that hockey would always be there for Logan, and if the medical bills got too high, he'd help us find a way to make sure he got to keep playing. It was the reminder I needed that my kids are surrounded by people who love them and are going to make sure they're okay, even if I can't be here.

Unfortunately, that was the perfect reminder that I might not be here, so I had to go cry some more. In retrospect, I should have had this stage of my life sponsored by Kleenex.

On Sunday, I went for my spine MRI and ran into a little trouble. The MRI tech struggled to start my IV, which isn't a surprise since I have terrible veins. She told me she wouldn't stick me more than twice. Now, normally, I am a pretty chill patient. I don't like to ask for anything, I will *not* push the call button for a nurse. You can have the resident give me a lumbar puncture in the ER, but at this point in time, I hadn't eaten or slept well in three weeks. My meeting with the neurosurgeon was the first thing in morning, and my spine was where we *knew* something was. I may or may not have yelled at this poor woman and told her she would stick me as many times as it took, or I would get on YouTube and insert my own IV. (But I did.) It was not one of my finer moments, but waiting is not your friend when it comes to things like this, and I couldn't wait anymore.

Monday morning was my birthday. Thirty-three is supposed to be an auspicious year. Thirty-three is tied to the two triangles of the Star of David. The Rig Veda describes thirty-three deities. There are thirty-three sensual heavens in Buddhism. Jesus lived thirty-three years and performed thirty-three miracles. (Did I mention I have a degree in religious studies and know lots of random facts?) Anyway, we headed in to see Dr. Nayar, nervous, but hopeful that Lisa was right and it wasn't in my brain. Dr. Nayar told us the radiologist hadn't looked at my spine MRI yet, but that my brain looked beautiful. What a relief! This was definitely something to celebrate. That night, we had lemon curd with berries, which is pretty much the best thing on earth. I refused to eat anything with white flour in it, and my mom managed to find a low-sugar recipe for the lemon curd and made it organic—and when I blew out my candle (it was a giant leftover Hanukkah candle) my kids asked me what I wished for, and I could tell them honestly, "Nothing."

On Friday, we saw my oncologist. She walked in and asked what the neurosurgeon told us. We explained he'd only told us my brain was clear. Her exact words were: "So, it's not good." We went from the high of "no brain involvement" to pretty darn low in the three seconds it took her to say that. She went on to explain that what she saw was a few larger tumors and then a "spray" of cells that looked like someone had shot paint at my spine with a straw. I heard "weeks or months, not years," but my husband heard "not weeks, but months or years," but either way, the message was that this was not going away—it was terminal. Austin asked out flat out if there was any possibility of it going away and was told no.

My oncologist told us that we should consider a clinical trial at National Institutes of Health and she'd already sent an email to Mark Gilbert. I interrupted her to tell her I already knew who Dr. Gilbert was (he's an ependymoma superstar who runs CERN and, while he was at MD Anderson Cancer Center, was directly responsible for saving the lives of at least five ependymoma patients whose stories I've read, and probably countless others who didn't write their stories down.)

We left the oncologist's office to meet with the radiation oncologist we'd met previously. We liked him better this time, but we left Georgetown feeling defeated and uncertain. The neurosurgeon felt it was too dangerous to operate or even biopsy because of location and the fact that I wasn't having any trouble walking or using the bathroom (which surprised everyone!). He didn't want to add symptoms if I wasn't having them already. The oncologist felt certain we could push him into doing it if we really wanted a biopsy. The radiation oncologist wanted to do limited lower spine-only radiation so I could have chemo later, with the limited approach hopefully sparing some of my bone marrow so I could have the blood counts necessary for chemotherapy. Again, the oncologist felt we could push him to do full spine. I didn't want to have to push my doctors. I wanted them to have a plan and for us to follow it. We left it that we would return in a few weeks after speaking to Duke, and NIH, where Dr. Gilbert now practices.

At home, I went from depressed to non-functional. I called Duke to check in with my radiation oncologist, but I found out later the message he received was "Kristina sent scans." That wasn't out of the ordinary because since ependymoma patients are so rare, I sent Dr. Kirkpatrick my scans every time I got one. The adjective "bad" would have let him know to call me immediately, but since that wasn't the message he got, he didn't realize it was a crisis. I reached out to Lisa and begged her to help me get in touch with Duke. Since I'd made them work with my Georgetown oncologist the last time, I didn't really have a firm relationship with the medical neuro-oncologist down there. Lisa reached out to Dr. Friedman and explained the situation and asked him to please give me a call because I was not handling things very well.

After Lisa told me she contacted Dr. Friedman, I held on to my cell phone like it was a doorframe and I'd just come off the Titanic. When he finally called, we had a thirty-second conversation that went something like this: "Hi, this is Henry Friedman from Duke. I'm at the airport. Screw everybody that thinks you're dying. I don't even think these are very good scans. I'm not saying we can cure you, but we'll fight like hell with you, and good things happen at Duke. I made you appointments for Friday. We've got a good plan, and we will take good care of you."

You're going to be shocked, but I sobbed.

Dr. Friedman, slightly perturbed, said, "Everything I just said is a good thing—why are you crying?" I tried to man up and explain to him I'd been waiting to hear someone tell me they had a plan and would fight with me. I wanted to hear there was hope. Luckily, that's right in the Duke Brain Tumor Center's tag line: "At Duke, There is Hope."

Telling the Kids ... Again

I will be up front here and let you know that I let my husband tell the kids the second time, too. I will note (with zest) that this time there was no way I should have told them because I was too shell-shocked from my appointment to tell them with any type of calm or assurance. It was definitely a relief for them to know because having to fake digestive issues to run in the bathroom and cry when they inadvertently broke my heart saying something like "I'm so glad about Silver Sparkles this year because you're all better," was getting a little old. At least now I could be honest that something was wrong in Wonderland.

When we arrived back from Georgetown, my mom was already at our house with the kids. Austin went in and I sat in the car and sang along to some old 90s boy band music.

C'mon, you know I cried.

I cried my eyes out over the unfairness of not getting to let my children have a fantasy childhood unaffected by pain or fear. I cried over the what-ifs of not seeing them grow up. I cried over the fact that they were crying, yet again, because of me. After about ten minutes, they came out to the car to get me, to hug me, to wrap their little broken hearts around mine. Logan came first, bent over from the pain of knowing he had to do this again. Savannah came second with Austin on one arm and reaching out for me with the other. Riley came next trying to stand tall and look courageous because he's the big brother and was thirteen, but with tears streaming down his determined face. My mom stayed inside and cried alone for a moment so she could try to recover from her own pain and shock. I have to pause for a moment to say I can't imagine the pain that this has all been for her because the thought of one of my children being diagnosed with something like a brain tumor keeps me up at night. I am not sure I could throw myself into helping them survive with no regard for how much pain I was feeling, which she has done not once, but twice.

I hugged my children and I promised them that no matter what we were going to look for the good things—for the blessings—and even on the worst days, we would find them and hope would keep us going. It was all I had to offer them at that point—the idea there would be good days even in the bad months to come, and that those bright spots might be enough to help us see the light at the end of the tunnel.

The problem was I still wasn't sure if that light was sunlight or an oncoming train.

Back to Durham

When we got to Duke, we waited a long time to see Dr. Annick Desjardins, which was not unusual. She tends to be off-schedule because her patients are complicated, but I would have waited days in that waiting room to hear what she told me. When she and her nurse, Rosemary, came into the room she took one look at me and said, "Somebody scared you. What happened?" I recapped how difficult things had been for me and how I was scared to eat and scared to sleep and scared to use deodorant because people just kept sending me "things" that caused cancer. I told her about my previous visits, and then she handed me a tissue.

"I am not scared of this tumor," she said.

Dr. Desjardins explained all of the good things that were happening. The tumor hadn't recurred in my brain stem, which is what we'd treated before with radiation, which made her think it was the type of ependymoma that responds particularly well to radiation. The tumor hadn't recurred in my brain at all, in fact, and she had patients who lived with spinal ependymomas for years and years and years. Finally, she'd seen those tumors melt away with the right treatment. I handed her a list of drugs I'd found in clinical trials as far away as Boston, and she told me she had access to all these drugs and could use them however I needed to make me better. Her plan would begin with Temodar and radiation, and then we'd see where we were. We could do more Temodar, or move on to Carboplatin and Avestin. We could even move up to immunotherapy drugs, if we found it necessary. She had a plan for a long game, if we needed it, although she'd still seen tremendous results with radiation.

"I have a plan, and fear is not part of the plan. I have your back," she concluded. "Metaphorically, and actually about the back."

Those words were so precious to me. They words were spoken to me before by people who encouraged me on the way, and having a doctor say them gave me more hope than I thought possible. Now, I'd love to tell you that hope was enough to pull me out of the deep pit I found myself in, but that would be a lie. Most cancer centers I've been to have you fill out a "Mental Distress" form of some type, and then I think they throw them out or use them to note what percentage of cancer patients have mental distress. I'm not really sure. In addition to looking at my form, Dr. Desjardins looked at me and took the time to say that post-traumatic stress was not uncommon in someone who was given a recurrent diagnosis, and that my brain needed a little help making serotonin so I could be happy. She needed me to be happy, healthy, and strong for treatment, so it would be good if I could start on a little something to help me. The grace with which she told me I needed help made me not feel like a failure, and the medication really helped me. Within a few weeks, I was able to focus on good things and direct my thoughts away from fear and distress. It didn't "fix" me, it just helped me get back to myself so I could turn my thoughts to positivity the way I had before. If you're in a similar situation, or heck, even a totally different situation, don't be ashamed or embarrassed to ask for help dealing with your emotions.

We met with Dr. Kirkpatrick, still fantastic, and he explained to us his plan. Duke's neurosurgeon, Dr. Alan Friedman (don't get confused, there's two Dr. Friedmans at Duke!) felt he could get a sample. If the tumor was anaplastic/grade III, then they would target the bottom part of my spine down into an area called the cauda equina, literally "horse hairs," where the nerves in your back are gathered kind of like a horse's tail, but in my case, where it was caked with tumor cells kind of like a tail coated in mud. This allowed me to have more chemo later. If it was grade I or grade II, they would irradiate the entire spine with the goal of treating anywhere the tumor might be thinking about going, too. We loved that everyone was on the same page. We loved that they weren't scared, and we loved being back at Duke. I sound like a fangirl during basketball season, I know, but I was so happy to be back in Durham. We set up treatment and waited to hear about a surgical date.

When we got home, we did go to NIH to have a consultation/third opinion. NIH's complex is a little different to get into than a typical hospital because it is a government facility. We had to show ID to get onto the campus, but once we were in, everyone was kind and friendly. The admin who checked us in asked about something that ended with me mentioning my faith, and she took the time to pray with us before we went up. So sweet. Dr. Gilbert and his team were amazing, and they recommended a course of proton therapy with no Temodar, which was a lower toxicity option, and proton therapy really is the new amazing thing in radiation therapy. NIH didn't have a machine, but Dr. Gilbert offered to enroll me in their outcomes study and set me up for treatment in Maryland on their proton machine. He echoed the feeling that my tumor type must be radiation-sensitive. He said he especially wanted me to do proton therapy because they'd expect me to live a long time, so if we could limit side effects, that was something he thought was worthwhile.

As crazy as it sounds, I wanted the Temodar and radiation. I thought about it the whole way home from NIH. I told Austin that at the end of treatment I needed to be able to look myself in the mirror and say that I came at this thing with everything I had and if it was still there, I obviously did everything I could have possibly done. If I did the radiation therapy or the partial spine radiation, I would beat myself up if the ependymoma was still there at the end of treatment because I could have done more.

I Plead No Contest to the Charge of Not Participating

There is a group of people on social media using various platforms to increase awareness and connection for people with brain tumors using the hashtag #BTSM (brain tumor social media). One of the topics of conversation that comes up frequently is how to get more people engaged in clinical trials. This is a difficult thing in brain tumors because, as I mentioned, it gets less money and the survival time is typically not very long. Finding treatment seems like a race against the clock from the get-go. At the same time, there is this concept that exists in the minds of some people, me included, that clinical trials make you a guinea pig.

I'm not ready to be a guinea pig yet.

I understand that a lot of people, I think my original oncologist included, consider my decision not to pursue a clinical trial to be incredibly selfish. Generally speaking, I consider the thoughts, feelings, needs, and emotions of everyone around me before I consider myself.

Generally speaking, I want to do the utilitarian thing, the thing that is for the greater good. Generally speaking, I am the type of person that would want my life to have meaning because I made it possible for other people to live. I sent Lisa a picture of my Temodar the first day I took it with a thank you message for her first husband. He is part of the reason I have this drug in the first place. His life allows mine to continue.

However, I have a lot of problems with clinical trials, especially where brain tumors are concerned. First and foremost, I have a strong problem with control groups. Duke, for example, has had tremendous success with its polio trial, but other centers always note there was no control group in its phase one trial. Why does there need to be a control group not receiving treatment? I understand the placebo effect, but you guys, we know what happens to glioblastoma patients. They die. They die quickly. Why aren't we able to use documentation regarding the typical response to existing protocols as the control against novel treatments and then give everyone the new treatment if it is working?

Next, I have a problem with the fact that clinical trials don't seem to be offering all that much where ependymomas are concerned. Of the clinical trials available to me at the time I was researching them, only eight were being offered and six of them were the same trial at different locations. I'm not sure if their momma didn't tell them about not putting their eggs all in one basket, but it seems like they didn't get the memo.

Finally, the reason I select doctors and treatment centers is because I want to be treated like a person, a competent person who is able to be involved in my care. I don't want to be a subject just yet. Enrolling in a clinical trial can also change who's treating you. NIH was willing to work to coordinate my care with my Georgetown doctors, but was unwilling to work with Duke. I don't know what the backroom politics of all that was, but I knew I wanted to go with the doctors who made me feel the best.

Some people really looked down on me not participating in a trial, but at the end of the day I needed to choose the course that felt the best for me. If you're eligible for a trial, and frequently comorbidities would exclude you, and the trial feels like the best option, by all means enroll! Help those coming after you. However, if no trials make you feel like they're your best option, rest secure in the fact that only 3 to 5 percent of cancer patients enroll in trials, and your choice of where to receive care is not going to be the difference between curing all cancer and everyone around you dying.

Laminectomy

The procedure I underwent at Duke was a laminectomy. That's fancy doctor-speak for "slice open your spine and get some tumor." I recovered in the hospital for a few days since they opened the dura—the thin, skin-like covering that keeps your cerebrospinal fluid where it's supposed to be. They needed me to lie flat for several days so it could heal. The procedure didn't take long, especially compared to my craniotomy, and the recovery wasn't bad either. They didn't even use sutures. They used a fancy purple super glue to hold my back together. I wasn't allowed to swim or bathe for a while, but it was no big deal. During the surgery, someone came out to tell Austin they were fairly sure that it was a grade III tumor, but that it's hard to tell when it's not frozen. We later found out it was actually grade II, which was great news because we could treat it more aggressively, and since we couldn't operate (first choice for ependymomas), at least our second-best option could be used to its fullest extent.

When I envisioned this surgery, I thought it was going to be some kind of laparoscopic procedure and I'd be in-and-out same day. It ended up being a four-inch incision that required me to lie flat for at least two days, and then possibly up to a week if Dr. Friedman didn't have warm fuzzy feelings about my dura closing well. Lying on your back for forty-eight hours is not fun. You can't even watch TV and I spent most of my time trying to gently flip myself from one side to another when different parts of my body went numb. If anyone out there needs an idea to win money on *Shark Tank*, I'd like to suggest a giant spatula that connects to hospital beds and flips patients, so they don't feel like such jerks asking people to constantly help flip them and move pillows. We had to stay in the area for two to three more days to make sure I didn't leak spinal fluid once I was up. Recovery in a hotel is not fun, but the whole thing was nothing compared to the craniotomy.

I really didn't require much in terms of recovery or physical therapy for the back surgery. I took it easy for a few weeks and only bent as far as I felt comfortable, which meant people had to fetch the Tupperware from the bottom shelf for me, but I learned to squat, rather than bend at the waist, which is supposed to be better for you anyway. My back was tired, fatigued, but it didn't hurt that much unless I pushed it too far.

If you are undergoing a cancer diagnosis push for the biopsy. The thing about surgeons is they are just a little bit narcissistic, so there is someone out there who thinks they are good enough to get a chunk of that sucker out of you. If your first surgeon can't get it, keep looking. If we had gone with everyone's hunch, including mine, we would have given up on treating more of my spine because we were all working on the assumption that I had a grade III. Knowing for sure we had a grade II tumor allowed us to fully use the radiation, and with the tumor-mapping capabilities now available from companies like Caris Molecular Intelligence Profiling, having some of the tumor available for testing can give your doctor additional information to help you have the right treatment, the right medicine, and the right approach for your best possible outcome.

In addition to helping you by giving you more information, I have heard too many stories from people who didn't get the biopsy up front only to find out later they were not being treated for the right thing. This is especially true in brain tumors. It is impossible to diagnose from an MRI—you can guess the type based on location, and you can guess on grade based on size or invasiveness, but you can't know for sure without taking a frozen sample to a microscope. As Green Day said, "Know Your Enemy."

Then We Blasted That Mother. Again.

Six weeks of daily radiation meant we were moving back to Durham—again. As I mentioned before, one of the first things the kids wanted to confirm was that we weren't going to leave them for six weeks again while we went to Duke for treatment. Austin was able to find a nice house about nine minutes from the cancer center that would accommodate our whole family, plus grandma, who was in charge of homeschooling—again.

That word, again, gets really old, really fast.

Before we moved to Durham, I needed a few preliminary things done. First of all, I needed something to make sure I was lined up correctly during treatment. Thankfully, that was not a mask this time, however it was a full-body "cradle." While I typically don't ask for pain killers, I remembered how badly it hurt last time when something was being formed on my body when I still had a surgical scar, so they gave me some medication before sending me in. This was a very good thing because typically, you'd need to buy me at least a few drinks before I'd take it all off in a room full of people, and that was what they asked me to do.

Once naked, I laid down on what I can only describe as a beanbag mattress. Four people inflated it with some kind of foam and pushed it around me. They drew all over me with permanent markers to the point where I looked like a 2-year-old's wall drawing, which they covered with stickers so I wouldn't wash them off. I guess that's better than getting radiation guidance tattoos, which is what a lot of people end up with. After that, I had an MRI in the exact position of the cradle in very, very small "cuts." MRIs take pictures in "slices" of your body, and this means the pictures of my spine were very thin and close together, so they would have as much detail as possible.

Finally, the day came to move down to Durham and start my real treatment. The house was snug but adorable, and everyone was happy to be together. The weirdest part about my treatment was taking the Temodar. Since I was on an oral chemo regimen, that meant I held a toxic, radioactive pill in my hand and then gave it to myself on purpose. It's definitely a strange feeling knowing you're poisoning yourself—taking that first pill felt internally a little like when you're anticipating something you know is dangerous or painful such as waiting to crest a roller coaster hill or anticipating the icy water hitting your body before you jump in.

Amazingly, my daily schedule, which became dominated by my treatment, did well with my body. I had to eat a certain number of hours before my Temodar, which happened an hour after my anti-nausea meds and my Dexamethozone, which had to go with food. Fun! The Temodar also had to be a certain amount of time before the radiation since we were using it as a radiation sensitizer. Thankfully after the first week, my schedule was generally the same, so I could at least plan my life out around a standard radiation time. I didn't get tired. I didn't get "sunburn" from the radiation. I didn't lose my hair from the Temodar or throw up. My worst symptoms? A daily headache in the afternoon, which ended up being from the Zofran I was on for nausea and in the fifth week of radiation, I started getting some incredibly painful heartburn because my esophagus was getting burned by the radiation.

(Note on Medication: I highly recommend labeling the top of your medication bottles with inspiration. I labeled my Zofran "Don't Yarf," my Temodar "Kill, Kill, Kill the Ependymoma," my Dexamethasone "'Roids" with a picture of a hulked-out arm, and my Sertraline "Be Happy." Not only does it make it easier to grab the correct bottle from your bag, it gives you a little smile.)

Since I don't usually call my doctors, I had to laugh when I finally called to ask what I could take for the heartburn. It was so bad it was keeping me up at night and I couldn't drink cold liquids or eat hot foods, so I finally called the nursing line. I knew what over-the-counter medications were available, but I didn't want to take anything without asking permission since I was on several other medications at the time. I talked to the nurse and explained my issue, and she said she would pass it on to my care team. Within three minutes, I got a call back from my radiation oncology nurse, the resident on my case, and Dr. Kirkpatrick. They all more or less expressed that since I never complain, when they heard I had called, they decided I must be dying. The resident did give me a prescription for liquid lidocaine, which I'm sure would work great if it didn't taste like what I'd imagine licking paint thinner tastes like, and if you could actually "drink it from a straw" like the bottle suggests. It's incredibly thick and the dose is too small to actually come up the straw before you're just sucking air. I ended up carrying around a bottle of vanilla cream Mylanta in my cancer center bag, which gave me a pretty good laugh, because my grandmother used to keep a bottle of Mylanta in her purse and just take a little hit of it the way someone might sneak a nip out of the flask in their purse. After a few days of

Pepcid and Mylanta, I was able to drink iced beverages again, and since tepid food and drinks are the bane of my existence (pick a temperature team and get on it), I was ready to finish treatment.

Mercifully, my weekly bloodwork was always pretty good. My platelets, even on spinal radiation and Temodar, stayed in the normal range almost the entire time, dipping just under normal only once. That did not, however, mean I was totally good to go. I tried to shave my legs part way through treatment and bled everywhere. The package insert did say it was a bad idea, but I didn't listen. My skin and blood were so thin. Be ye not so dumb and get waxed or something if you're worried your radiation team is judging you for your hairy legs.

P.S. They're not looking.

A Few Thoughts on Side Effects, or Dear Pharma Researchers

You know what's totally jacked up about the side effects you have to undergo from chemo and radiation? They don't work the way they should. Now, I know what you're thinking "Kristina, honey, side effects don't usually 'work the way you want them to.'" I totally understand that, in principle, but I think the pharmaceutical researchers are missing out on some really big opportunities here.

For example, in the area of hair loss, if some drug company could come up with a way to target their side effects a little better, they could really stand to make some money! My mom's friend, April, warrior princess, lost her eyebrows and they never grew back. You know who wants to have to get eyebrow tattoos? Nobody. I can pull handfuls of hair out of my hairbrush every day, although due to my ridiculously thick hair, I'm not bald. I can also wipe the tiny hairs off the trunk of my body because they're falling out. You know who wants to do either of those things? Nobody. In the meantime, there's a warning label included with my Temozolomide telling me not to shave with a razor because my skin is so thin that I'll be a bloody mess. I know what you're thinking, *"Your skin can't possibly be that thin. They're just being overly cautious!"* I know, because I thought that, too, and I ended up cutting off every goose bump on my legs and bleeding everywhere. EVERYWHERE. Now, what can we learn from this lesson?

If you said, "Listen to your medicine inserts," the answer is no. You should have already learned that.

We learned that chemotherapy should target unwanted body hair. I want fabulously hair-free legs and underarms—I do not want a fabulously bald head, clogged sink, or to have to use a stencil on any part of my face that is not for a glitter tattoo.

Radiation is a similarly big letdown. I've had radiation twice now, and here is a list of things that I do not currently do to the best of my knowledge:

- Glow in the dark
- Sling webs from my fingertips
- Move things with my mind
- Fly
- Mutate into another animal
- Really, anything cool at all that would get me a superhero franchise

Understanding that maybe becoming a superhuman mutant half-breed might be too big of an ask, even for Duke, I was willing to settle for some light cosmetic work. I tried asking my radiation oncologist if we could work it out so that my radiation patterns sculpted my eyebrows and permanently removed any stray lady-mustache hairs. He was not as amused as I was by this question. I did get some weird hair loss on my head with a giant rectangle missing in the back and some wavy stripes down the side. Mostly, the things they warned me about with radiation bit the big one. They included (and this is a mixed list from spine and brain) the potential for:

- Incontinence (that's right—diaper time!)
- Memory loss
- Temporary paralysis
- Muscle damage
- Nerve damage
- Internal organ damage

None of these things are on my Top 10 List of "Awesome Things I'd Like to Happen." I'm not saying they need to make radiation and chemotherapy so awesome that everyone wants to do them. I'm just saying, if we're going to make hair fall out, can't it at least be from somewhere I'd like to shave if my skin wasn't crepe-paper thin? We can be fair to the guys, too, and maybe target that little patch on the back that sticks out awkwardly on tank tops.

Not a sermon, just a thought.

Home Again, Home Again, Jiggity Jig

The hardest part of being in Durham was being way from our support system, but we were again incredibly blessed by the people who loved us keeping that feeling strong, even from a distance. My Bible study group sent us down with money for food and gas, my friends kept a steady stream of cards and notes coming (and mail is my love language!), people sent nausea aids even though I didn't need them. Love poured down from everywhere. From notes and puzzles for my kids to boxes of fruits and vegetables from my godmother, Beth, people made sure we knew we might be far away, but we were never alone. I even got visits from two friends who were either passing through or just made it a point to come down. One of them was the best cancer buddy ever, Jennifer. She came down for the purpose of giving me a hug, watching Netflix with me, and taking a nap with me on the sofa. I tried to entertain her, and she just looked at me and said, "Hey, buddy. You look sleepy. I'm going to get us pillows." She's got cancer friend skills.

We finally finished up treatment and my doctors were pleased with how I did. I waited at home for a few weeks to let the radiation swelling, which looks like tumor on an MRI, go down. I spent most of my time sleeping when we got home. The exhaustion wasn't as bad as my brain radiation, but I was definitely tired and needed lots of sleep. I was a little less harsh on myself this time as far as getting back to my normal routine, which I think helped a lot. I kept walking during treatment, and did that when I got home, too, and then each day added in a little more activity, whether it was helping to teach the kids something or answering emails for a few minutes.

On June 6, Austin and I left for Durham around 3 a.m. for a new MRI, appointments with my oncologist and radiation oncologist, and bloodwork. Both doctors were very happy with the outcome, but Dr. Desjardins opted to start me on a year of chemotherapy. The good news made me happy, but I knew that meant we hadn't gotten everything. They offered me the option of daily oral chemotherapy at a lower daily dose, or one week a month at a higher daily dose. I liked the idea of the Temodar poking at any remaining ependymoma cells every minute of every day, similar in my mind to the way my boys treat each other when they're riding in the back seat of the car next to each other. My younger son always claims that if his brother doesn't stop touching him he's going to jump out of the car window—and I'm hoping the ependymoma will take the same approach and just leave.

I won't miss it when it's gone.

Recovery Part Deuce

I have to pat myself on the back a little and say I was a total boss at full spine radiation. I killed it. If there was a gold medal for spine radiation, I would have won it. I took more naps, but I was otherwise good. I didn't have any of the potentially devastating side effects they warned me about—from early onset menopause to loss of mobility. I did a great job. I felt pretty good most of the time, too, except for those Zofran headaches.

For some reason, though, when we got home, I was a hot mess. I was sleeping from around 8:30 p.m. to 12:30 p.m. and yes, I mean that I literally went to bed when my children did and slept until lunch. Then I usually took a little nappy around 4:00 p.m. to 6:00 p.m. As soon as I weaned off of the "baby dose" of Decadron (steroid) I was on, which was just 1 milligram a day, I broke out in hives from head to toe. My face looked like a lobster, and eventually my skin broke open and bled. I didn't want to eat. I didn't want to walk. I didn't want to do anything but sleep, which I let myself do for a few weeks, and slowly that resolved and each day I pushed myself to do more and more—to help with school or help make dinner or walk a little further than the previous day. By July, though, I'd been out of treatment for about two months, and was sleeping from around 11:00 p.m. to 7:00 a.m., and while I felt fatigued faster, I could go about my day like a fairly normal person. I would say that about three months out I felt like a slightly older, but still awesome, version of myself.

My second time around, I did much better about giving myself grace when I said no to things. Our church emailed me, along with all the previous years' VBS volunteers, and I knew I couldn't help in-person, but I offered to help prep materials if they needed me to, or to come in and make copies. It ended up not being something they needed, but I didn't beat myself up over the fact that I had to say no. I knew from the last time I recovered that I'm not saying no forever, I'm just saying no right now. I've learned the currency you have to spend that matters is time. The funny thing about this particular currency is you don't know how much of it you have. It's a little bit like going on a spending spree at Target and checking out one item at a time not knowing when you're going to overdraft your account. Some of us are acutely more aware that we might be approaching our spending limit, while others are blissfully ignorant of the fact that they're about to hit that wall hard. I wouldn't quite go so far as the song that says it hopes you get the chance to live like you're dying, but I will say once you are aware you might hit empty at any point on your account, Dave Ramsay himself couldn't make you do a better job budgeting your time.

I decided to take it easy on myself for the next year and not take on teaching a class at our science co-op, which I love doing, but I love other things more. I ordered an 18-month Erin Condren planner online on the night before my repeat MRI when I couldn't sleep from the anxiety of worrying about the next day. The ad popped up on the website I was on, and I originally just played around with the colors and layouts, but I ended up finding one I loved with part of Joshua 1:9 on it: "Be Strong and Courageous." I set it up with a grey background—my power color—and as I went to check out, the site popped up and asked me if I would like to change from a 12-month planner to an 18-month planner, and despite that I was now spending $50 on an impulse-buy, I clicked yes because I was planning on having all of that time in my account, and I was going to use it on things that made me happy to write in pen.

Some days were still really hard, and because I am actually in my thirties and not eighty, I sometimes forget I'm delicate. I got shingles, which I thought was only for older people, and then that turned into an infection because my skin was thin and my body was so busy dealing with my daily chemotherapy regimen that it couldn't fight like it used to. Paper cuts took weeks to heal, and especially when I had the shingles, the pain was a lot to deal with. But staying focused on things that make me truly happy and proud to spend my time budget on helped me deal with getting through recovery this time, too.

My Friend Has Cancer and I Don't Want to Suck: A General Guide

It is amazing to me the things people say when they're not sure what to say, or when they think they're helping. Here's a general rule. If you don't know what to say, don't say anything. Don't try to grasp for platitudes, don't try to solve the problem—unless you're an oncologist, in which case, please solve the problem. Here is a list of a few things to avoid telling people when they're diagnosed with cancer, all of which people actually said to me:

- I just feel like your headaches would go away if you lost some weight.
- Essential oils cure cancer, but the government doesn't want you to know.
- I would never let them poison my body with radiation. I would go to Mexico and do a macrobiotic diet and coffee enemas.

- My grandmother just died of cancer.
- My neighbor just died of cancer.
- I knew someone else who had brain cancer, and he only made it three weeks.
- Just you and your husband are going to Durham? Wow! It's like a little honeymoon! You're going to have so much fun!
- You look amazing! You've lost so much weight from the radiation! I hope you can keep it up!
- You're getting better every day! (This is especially hurtful in the middle of radiation when you're getting weaker every day.)
- Are you eating non-organic berries? Everyone knows GMOs and pesticides cause cancer.
- Are you drinking the city water? Fluoride causes cancer.
- Is that bread? Everyone knows carbs cause cancer.
- I bet that keeping your cell phone in your pocket gave you cancer.
- I read this article on the Internet about magic berries/government conspiracy/non-plastic-coated water bottles/coffee enemas/anything not published by a medical journal or actual cancer authority.

Generally speaking, your response to someone who has cancer should be: "This sucks, and I am sorry it's happening." If you wouldn't pursue the course they're pursuing, it is your job to keep your mouth shut because to be completely honest, you don't know what you're going to do until you're the one actually staring at the image on the screen being told that you're the one who's going to die if you do nothing. As far as all the Internet articles, you can find contradicting articles for anything. All you're doing with those is contributing to fear and self-blame for someone's sickness, and they really don't need that. By the time I got to Duke for my second diagnosis, I was only drinking non-BPA bottled PH balanced water and eating organic, non-GMO celery because even fruit had too much sugar. I was scared to put anything in my mouth, scared to use shampoo, scared to wear deodorant even if it was organic because it still had some additive people weren't sure about. Fear is already fighting on its own; you don't need to help it.

As far as what you *can* do for someone with cancer, or really, any kind of diagnosis (we had a lot of people that were totally amazing and helped us so much), if you really want to help, it's important you do it in a constructive way. Here are some do's and don'ts:

- DO be specific when you offer help. On top of being sick, the person does not need to come up with ideas for how to engage your blanket offer of "doing something." I would like to bring dinner next week on Wednesday, or I would like to come and clean your kitchen for you after church on Sunday is good. "Let me know if you need anything" just makes more work.

- DON'T just show up. I actually had someone show up twice unannounced, once when I was sleeping during recovery (she wanted me to be woken up because it was 11 a.m., not a normal time to be sleeping), and then again on a day when I was in so much pain I wanted everyone go away. Call first and schedule, and then call again day of to make sure they're still up to visitors.

- DON'T come if you or anyone in your household is sick. "I didn't bring the kids because they all have strep" is not you loving someone with a compromised immune system.

- DO ask permission. Some people might love to have a GoFundMe or public collection taken for them. I would have died of embarrassment, and actually asked for someone to stop as soon as I found out they'd done that the first time. The second time, my small group had an emergency fund and quietly gave us grocery money without setting up any sort of online sob story, and we were very thankful for that.

- DO stay in contact, but DON'T expect a response. I had wonderful people in my life who wrote me letters, emails, Facebook messages, and texts and would end them with "Don't need you to write back unless you're feeling up to it!" Some days I really wanted to talk, and some days I just wanted to sleep. Having the expectation of reciprocity removed was so helpful to me.

- DON'T assume "they'll just be thankful for anything." My family gave up white flour and sugar with me after my second round of cancer, and people saying they were going to bring dinner, ignoring that, and bringing spaghetti meant I had to find somewhere for the spaghetti to go. My grandmother would have come back from the dead and killed me for wasting food, and it meant I had to come up with a last minute backup dinner plan.

Lest you think I'm making any of this up, here's an actual message I had to put out there on my social media:

"You guys, I promise that when I feel up to visitors any time, I will let you know. Until then, PLEASE be patient and respectful of me. I am tired and achy, and I know I don't typically complain on Facebook, so you might not realize, but I do NOT NOT NOT want people just stopping by unannounced. You're likely to get me mid-nap, not dressed, not showered, or just plain ugly because I'm in pain. I am so sorry if you think I'm a big mean jerk, but I only have so much energy and I get to choose to spend it where I want. That means some days I may feel up to something (i.e., going to my Sunday School class) and some days I may not. That doesn't mean you get to decide what I am up for."

It was really hard for me to post that, but I'd actually had people get mad at me because if I did anything, like going to my church class, then I should be up to going to their barbeque, and that wasn't true. I had to choose very carefully where safe places were for me during recovery, and where I had enough energy to be. Sitting in class watching a video for an hour might be something I'm up to, but socializing with a large group of people I don't know might not be, and that's okay.

Now I know this has been kind of a downer, so I want to end with some unexpectedly amazing and awesome things that people did for me so that you can get ideas for how to be supportive, too. Here's some of the awesome I received:

- People that were hilarious. I think one of my favorite texts I received was: "It was extremely inconsiderate of your tumor to decide to come back during Lent when I can't be on Facebook. I mean, seriously." Letting me know you're interested in what's going on with me and are thinking about me in a way that makes me laugh will get you plus 10 points.

- Oscar, one of the dads on my son's hockey team lost his mother to cancer when he was very young, so I know my diagnosis and seeing my son going through that had to hit very close to home for him. Instead of telling me "my mom died of cancer when I was his age," he went with letting me know his dad's wife was having miraculous results with a clinical trial for her lung cancer. I will never, ever, forget the fact that he overlooked his own pain and chose to lift me up instead of commiserating with the fear.

- The same hockey dad, and Julia, a hockey mom, knew I loved dancing to the old school music they played between plays, and they made an extra effort to play 90s rap during the last game I got to watch before starting treatment. It made my day, and while it might have actually been for the kids, it meant everything to me.

- My lawyer friend Jennifer (aka, Cancer Friend Skills) wrote a hilarious legal notice informing my ependymoma that it was already served once with notice to vacate, and was now in breach of that. I have it up in my kitchen and love to read it as a reminder that this isn't welcome in my life.

- My friend Heidi took the time to find the most sarcastic and funny cancer cards she could. My favorite one read: "You know what, this sucks. I wish I had something better to say, but I don't. But I'm not going anywhere, so you'll just have to deal with that." Then on the inside she wrote me a Bible verse and some prayer encouragement. Knowing your audience is a great way to ensure your message is well-received.

Finally, if you screw up and you say something that you shouldn't have, recognize the power of saying you're sorry. I know people that have lived their entire lives with hurts that were inflicted upon them in a situation like this whether they were told that it was "better their mom was in heaven" or whether they were told that "God wouldn't give them more than they can handle" (P.S. Don't say either of those). There's power in asking for forgiveness and recognizing that you did it wrong. There's even more power in giving forgiveness and not having to hold on to people's words on top of what you're already facing.

So Where Are We Now?

At the time I'm writing this all down, it's winter of 2019, and I'm coming up on one year post-chemo. I remain cautiously optimistic that my MRIs have been amazingly clean. The idea of being a chronic cancer patient is a little strange for me. I joke with doctors that aside from the whole "brain tumor thing" I'm really healthy. Aside from being "fluffy," I have low blood pressure, great blood panels (when I'm not on chemo), and I don't even take a daily vitamin because we eat so many fresh fruits and vegetables. I've read stories, though, of people who have lived a long time with ependymomas, one for 17 years! I met a woman in the radiation oncology nursing area after getting my cradle formed—a pediatrician—who had been living with leptomeningeal metastases, my diagnosis the second time around, for seven years. She explained that she was often off chemo and they'd watch her disease and if it started getting uppity, she'd do a round of chemo and put it back in its place, and then keep going.

Stories like those inspire me. They give me hope I can keep going, too, and while I'm telling this story five years into the process of dealing with this ependymoma (anyone who calls your cancer diagnosis a "journey" and doesn't give you cruise tickets should get a throat punch), I feel like I'm just at the beginning. I don't know what the future will hold specifically, but I know I will keep going for as long as I can and for as long as my doctors will fight with me. I mentioned that the tag line at Duke is "At Duke There is Hope" and how that really resonated with me, but when I started with my original diagnosis, there was also hope inside of me, and that's what I'd like to leave you with, if you'll keep reading.

PART TWO

How'd We Get
Through This?

Caffeine and Jesus:
A Life Philosophy

Telling the story of my brain tumor without talking about God is really hard for me. You may have noticed that He snuck in a few times, but generally, I tried to remove most of the faith from my story up front, and that was on purpose. I wanted to tell my story so it could be read by anyone, but the facts and timeline are really only half of the story. They tell the "how" of making it through this process. God tells the 'why." Looking back at everything that's happened to me, it's completely covered in the fingerprints of God. If you want to know how I have managed to make it through this whole process, the answer is a lot of things: supportive family, compassionate friends, amazing doctors, advanced medications, but on top of that, a whole lot of Jesus.

There's a sign that sits on the counter in my kitchen that says, "All I need today is a little bit of coffee and a whole lot of Jesus." That's been true of this whole ependymoma process, too. Well, actually, what I needed was a little bit of Valium and a whole lot of Jesus. Surgery hurt. From the beginning to the place we are now, I can look at my life and see where different things have been orchestrated for my good. Could I look at these things and think they were giant cosmic coincidences or good luck? Sure, I could do that. However, for me, there are too many coincidences to believe they all happened at random, and it's hard to believe in good luck when you're looking down the barrel of your own mortality. So, let's start again, and let's go over how this whole thing happened with God in the driver's seat, and the lessons I was able to learn and the amazing faith moments that happened because I was willing to walk this path with God, even in the times I had to crawl. If you want to know how I continue to make it through this, the answer is pretty simple—I quit on day one.

Quitting Day One

Before my diagnosis, I worked as a children's minister for the Methodist church. I absolutely love working with children and telling them about Jesus: I know all the *Veggie Tales* songs; I own all the Max Lucado books; I can make a children's sermon object lesson using my purse and thirty seconds of prep time. I did not, however, love working for churches. It's not that it made me hate church or hate God, it's just once you've seen how the sausage gets made, it can be really hurtful if you don't have the proper spiritual backing, and I didn't. By the time I stopped working for churches, I was in a place where I was really questioning God and his plan for my life and what I was supposed to think about church and faith and his relationship with me.

In worship one day in late November 2012, we sang the song *Show Me Your Glory* by Jesus Culture and I really prayed that song. It's based on Exodus 33:18 where Moses is speaking to God and asks for God to reveal himself to him. In that passage, the Lord tells Moses He will make

His goodness pass before him and proclaim the name of the Lord before him. There's specifically a part of the song where you repeat the phrase "I'm not afraid" and at that point in praying the song, I stopped dead in my tracks and had a conversation with God. It was three words in response to the song's declaration of not being afraid. Just three words, and I answered them without hesitation. The words were:

Are You Sure?

Yes, I was sure! I wanted my relationship with God to be stronger. I wanted to see His glory. I wanted to step into the cloud. I wasn't afraid. God could bring it on. Does that mean that I think God gave me a brain tumor? No, it doesn't, and honestly, ependymomas are so slow-growing that mine was probably there for years to get as big as it was. Does it mean I asked God to show me His glory and He used my circumstances to do it? Yes, it does. When I got that initial phone call telling me I had a brain tumor, in spite of the tears and the trying to figure out if ependymoma started with an a or an e so I could look it up on the internet, I was able to hear clearly those same words again in my heart:

Are You Still Sure?

And the thing was, my answer hadn't changed. I was still sure that I wanted to see what God could do. I wanted to see His glory, and if this was the situation that was going to show it to me, then I was still all-in. There's a phrase we use in Christianity, "The peace that surpasses understanding," which comes from Philippians 4:7. "And the peace of God, which surpasses all understanding, will guard your hearts and your minds in Christ Jesus." I never understood that phrase until the night I learned I had a brain tumor. While I was upset and definitely shed tears with my husband as we tried to wrap our minds around what was about to come, I had a supernatural sense of well-being in my soul that told me I could trust God to handle this situation, and so, rather than turning myself into a "warrior" or a "conqueror" or declaring on Facebook that

I was going to "tackle," "fight," or "destroy" my tumor, I did the exact opposite.

I quit.

Now, that probably sounds a little strange. You've already read my story, so you know we sought out the best possible doctors and multiple opinions. You know I cried tears and so did my family. Quitting didn't mean I was giving up my right to experience the emotions of the situation around me, it meant I didn't have to worry because worry wasn't going to help me in any way, shape, or form. Quitting meant waving the white flag to God and letting him know that I was fully aware this was too big for me to carry and that He was going to have to do it for me. I walked smiling into brain surgery because I gave up my future to God. I gave up control to God. I gave up thinking I could heal myself or fix myself or do anything for myself to God. I would do everything that was in my power to do—I would go to the appointments and find the doctors and I would show up for physical therapy and radiation and I would put in the work, but God would have to carry the burden for me.

My friend Jennifer, of Netflix and nap fame, and I have a saying: "You don't need permission." For us, it's a reminder that we are allowed to claim ownership of our situation without permission from anyone outside of ourselves. I mention that because quitting the "fight" before I even started was me giving God permission to handle it and to show me His glory, just like I asked. He didn't need my permission, but I was giving it to Him, anyway, and that surrender was what He was looking for.

If you'd like another way of looking at what I did, Shaun Alexander, former Seahawks MVP, was on our local Christian radio station one day. I actually sat in my car and listened to his entire interview rather than going in to get my coffee because what he was saying was so good and so true, and resonated with my story. He was talking about pressure to perform and to accomplish and he said, "Stress comes from not believing God is big enough to fill in my gaps. If I've got five and pressure says I need six, I say, 'God, I'm gonna give you five and trust you for six.' If pressure says I need 100 and I've only got five, I say, 'God, I'm going to give you my five, and if you want this to happen, I'm going to trust you for the other ninety-five." I told God I would give him what I had, which was to show up. He was going to have to do everything else because I was just totally incapable. He was going to have to be the Father in a big way.

I'm not generally a fan of applying every verse in the Bible to my own situation. That doesn't mean I don't think it's all true and valid, it's just I'm not a fan of naming and claiming every verse where God is talking to David or Moses or Paul as my own. I mean, if we did that, men would be in big trouble every time they ticked off a woman who took Judges 4:21 as a life verse. (Helpful hint: that's the one where Jael kills Sisera with a tent stake in his sleep) However, I've found that in any situation I'm in, I'll find myself drawn to a verse that is supposed to be the one I hold on to for the situation I'm in. In this particular case, I held on to Isaiah 41:13 like a life raft. "For I the Lord your God will hold your right hand, saying to you, 'Fear not, I will help you.'" Just like I held the hands of my children and guided them through things they were not big enough to handle, God was going to hold my hand through this situation and guide me through it. I knew that with every fiber of my being. That didn't mean I knew that everything was going to be okay, quite to the contrary. I knew quitting and surrendering to God's will could mean any of a number of outcomes, but I also knew having peace with His control and His will meant I was allowing His power to be made perfect in my weakness, and as you've read in this story, I was very weak. But the Bible tells us something else, and that is that God's power is made perfect in our weakness. When it is abundantly clear that we are incapable of something, God is able to really show off what He can do. There is nothing I could have done to heal myself in this situation. There is no reason I should have been able to do anything I did—from smiling to walking out of the hospital in eight days—and that meant people could watch me, but see Him.

Because People are Watching

What I loved most about the peace God had given me was it allowed me to be a part of Him showing up and showing off. Being able to smile, be kind, and have peace allowed me to show there was something different happening inside of me than happened in most people in my situation. I had nurses, doctors, friends, and family who could watch and see that there was something inside of me that was different, and they wanted to know what it was. I planted myself firmly under the umbrella of God's protection, and I was loud and proud about the fact that I could trust Him. As I prepped for my first Silver Sparkles event, part of my media promotion was an interview on NBC Washington, and even they noted I was still smiling the night before brain surgery, showing a picture of me with my freshly-shaved head and an honest smile on my face. I was joyful because I wasn't carrying the burden. Now, before you think this interview went without incident, let me mention that when they asked if I was scared, I told them I decided early on that I was either going to have the surgery, wake up, and work hard to recover, or I was going to—no joke, this is verbatim—"Wake up, and give Jesus a fist bump."

Yes, I just described dying as waking up and giving our Savior a "What's up?" fist bump.

But that wasn't necessarily wrong because I feel like throughout this process, I've gotten some fist bumps from Jesus, and I didn't even have to go to Heaven to get them. When you're trying to evaluate your life, a lot of times it's really tempting to think that the bad things, the crisis situations, are endings. A breakup or divorce, a diagnosis, the death of a loved one— sometimes those things aren't the ending; they're a plot twist opening the door to more amazing things that are to come.

Looking back with that 20/20 hindsight people always talk about, I can see those plot twists were all for my good. I found myself unexpectedly pregnant at 19 and ended up moving with my new husband to finish school outside of D.C. where we could be close to supportive family. After radiation, I wouldn't have been able to have children. I got my babies early so I could have them at all. The move back home to finish school put me within driving distance of the doctors that saved my life again and again. Having cancer has given me some of the greatest joys of my life because people got to watch God moments happening in my life and to experience that joy and faith with me.

After my first diagnosis, my oldest son, Riley, decided to get baptized. No joke. You can actually watch his testimony (https://vimeo. com/104426057). That's a full-on mom brag. You can tell everything I've told you was true because this kid knows I was sick, knows it could come back, and knows I believed God had a plan for me, even if I died. Kids don't make this stuff up. God blessed my obedience to His call to trust Him in that He showed my son he could trust Him, too. I would do it all again to hear him say, "Hello, my name is Riley Kotlus, and I'm getting baptized because Jesus is the Lord of my life."

All the pain, all the uncertainty, all the recovery, it would all be worth it for that one thing.

At Passover, we sing a song called *Dayenu*, which translates to "it would have been enough." The song is a list of things that God did for the Jewish people: If He had rescued them from Egypt, but not punished the Egyptians, it would have been enough; If He had punished the Egyptians, but not parted the Red Sea, it would have been enough; and so on. I love singing this song with my family each year because it reminds me of how I came out of my first diagnosis feeling. If God had allowed me to have a successful surgery and have deficits to recover from, it would have been enough. If He allowed me to have no deficits and didn't allow me to tolerate radiation, it would have been enough. If He allowed me to tolerate radiation, but had no other purpose, it would have been enough. If He had a purpose for Riley to be baptized, and no one else ever saw His glory, it would have been enough. Luckily for the Jews in the wilderness, and for me, God is a God of abundance and He is constantly giving more than enough.

A little after Riley's baptism, one of my friends messaged me to tell me she wanted to go to some exploratory Christianity classes and wanted to know if I would go with her. We spent the next eight Tuesdays sitting in class for an hour or so, and then hitting the local IHOP until 1 or 2 in the morning to talk through what she'd just heard. Two days before my birthday, two years after my surgery, I got to watch my friend, Caitlin, be baptized. I would do it all again to hear her say, "Hello, my name is Caitlin, and I'm getting baptized because Jesus is the Lord of my life." All the pain, all the uncertainty, all the recovery, it would all be worth it for that one thing.

And the "one things" kept coming. I shared my testimony with people and got to see the faith of those around me multiplied, to know that people who hadn't prayed in years took a knee on my behalf and saw their prayers answered. I want to be very, very clear that none of those things were done by me—that was all God—but I got to be a part of that, and it was miraculous. The ironic part about it is that you would think just like the song, it would have been enough.

Finite Quantities

I already told you I didn't "battle" with my cancer. Our battles aren't with cancer—they're with the enemy who wants to pull us out of that umbrella of protection. Ephesians 6:12 makes it really clear: "Our struggle is not against flesh and blood, but against the rulers, against the authorities, against the powers of this dark world and against the spiritual forces of evil in the heavenly realms." The battle I had to fight was in my own mind.

Here was the thing—I lived once through tremendous obstacles and saw firsthand what God could do when I trusted Him. I knew God could be generous with time on this earth. I knew Hezekiah cried out to God and begged Him not to take his life, and God told him He'd heard his prayers and seen his tears and would add fifteen years to his life.

But here was the other thing—I knew Jesus cried out to God in the Garden of Gethsemane; that he cried until he bled, that he asked for any other way for salvation to happen, and that God told him no.

When I got my second diagnosis, I laid in bed like Hezekiah and cried out to God, but I had zero expectations of Him hearing me and giving me more time. In fact, I was sure I had used up all of the favor God could possibly have to give me. I'd maxed out grace. I'd maxed out miracles. I had withdrawn everything from my God account. I decided, for some reason, our infinite God was limited to finite quantities I could comprehend. How many times as a mom, as a daughter, as an employee, as a volunteer, had I found myself tapped out, especially of patience, and had nothing left to give?

Now, obviously, believing this lie was even dumber than deciding to go off the IV pain medication, but this was where I was vulnerable, and that's exactly where you get hit. I have always struggled with self-worth, and I was so completely overcome by all God had done for me before that I was willing to bite the apple and step out of His protection into the lie that He wouldn't do anything else for me. Once you step out of that protection, you're really vulnerable, and it can be a fast downward spiral. Once you're out of that umbrella of protection, you're a much easier target. This was how I landed into depression, not eating, not sleeping—and once you're not doing those things, well, then you're beaten. Not only was I mentally defeated, I was physically exhausted and in pain.

This time, I had to really pull myself up and put myself back into a place where I was mentally capable of handling what was happening to me. Medication helped—and I've already explained what an advocate I am of that—but serotonin on its own wasn't going to be enough, so I needed to surround myself with people that could speak truth to me, and to build my faith back up to the point where I could step back under that umbrella of protection, no matter what.

Even If You Don't...

The night before my craniotomy, I posted a message on Facebook to my friends. It read "I have every intention of waking up tomorrow after surgery and working to get better, but if I don't, God will still be God. Even if I am paralyzed, even if I die, God will still be God and He will still be good." I echoed that message every time I gave my testimony or told my story about my brain tumor, ending with, "We hope that it won't come back, but if it does, God will still be God, and He will still be good." When I look back at it now, I can see with my second diagnosis, I was being asked the same question I was the first time.

Are You Sure?

And the thing is, I was sure. I just needed to get back to basics. I needed to go back to my boys Shadrach, Meshach, and Abednego who walked into the fire and said, "Listen, our God can save us, but EVEN IF HE DOESN'T..." I needed to get back to where I knew my God was able to save me from any tumor, from any depression, from any problem big or small, but that the outcome might not be the one I wanted. The point was whether I hoped in Him for my life or trusted Him for life after death, but it needed to be well with my soul either way so I could leave it up to Him. Worrying never changed an outcome.

I may not have plans, but I definitely have outcomes in mind. This is an actual conversation between my husband and me:

> Austin: You're right. Things should always be the way you planned them in your head.
> Me: Nah, I don't usually have a plan.
> Austin: Right. Things should go exactly as you dreamed them up on the fly in your head.
> Me: My man—give me a high five.

I had to go back and not expect the outcome I wanted to the point of exhausting myself with worry because it wasn't going to change anything, and because God, unlike me, has a plan that goes all the way to the end of time.

To overcome where I was required a little something we like to not focus on called "Spiritual Discipline." The first time I was sick, for whatever reason, joy and peace and faith flowed through me with no effort on my part. This time, I was going to have to work for it. I needed to start with the hard truth that Jesus could have saved himself on the cross, but instead saved me. Grace wins. Love wins. Mercy wins. The central theme of our faith is hope rises from death. That means hope rises from whatever situation you find yourself in that you think is insurmountable. If I was worth dying for, then I was worth granting peace again (and whatever else God had in his plan for me because He is more than able and gives gifts abundantly to the point of giving us His own life). 1 Corinthians 2:10 tells us God gives us His spirit that searches diligently…even sounding the profound and bottomless things of God. God had no limits.

Next, I needed to change my mindset. In worship one Sunday, we were singing *Spirit of the Living God*, which caused me to ugly cry in a packed worship service with hundreds of people. Luckily, we go to a contemporary church and either to keep costs down or because it looks cool, they don't really turn the lights on. This song reminds us when God comes in it changes what we see, what we're seeking, and us. Knowing God was present in the situation and I could openly invite Him to have His way in my situation again, meant I could stop looking for bad news and death and pain. I could start looking for good things. When I got home, I was flipping through *Jesus Calling* and came back to February 15, which I read every day of treatment. This message said stop trying to limit God's greatness by telling Him what to do, but instead to focus on what He was already doing. I needed to let go of the future and to change my focus. I needed to stop being afraid of the dark and remember that I am a light, and the darkness is scared of me.

Choose Joy

Stormie Omartian says, "In the darkest times of your life, your praise should be the loudest. Let the enemy know you are not afraid of the dark." With my new perspective—knowing I needed to let God do what He was going to do, and I needed to focus on what He was already doing—I told my children how we were going to get through this second trial. I told them it is a choice to see the good every day. I told them it's a choice to identify every good and perfect gift as coming from God. I told them we were going to realize that the greatest good was God, and that meant every kind word, every happy occurrence, every inspiring "coincidence," and every glimmer of hope was God speaking to us. If watching God do what only He could do would change what we see and what we seek, we were going to do the reverse and start seeing and seeking what He was doing right now.

It's a choice to see joy. Choose it.

The verse I grabbed onto this time was Ephesians 3:14-21. It's the conclusion of Paul's prayer for the gentiles to know how deep and how wide and how high the love of Christ is, and that God, who is able to do immeasurably more than we can ask or imagine according to His power that is at work within us, would have glory.

We started this daily praise practice in the most basic way we could. Every night, before we prayed as a family, I would ask everyone what their blessing was for the day. We practiced seeing God. The kids were much better at it than I, but that was okay. Their faith and their sight helped me to wash the jadedness from my eyes. Starting with joy and gratitude was a lifestyle change in the season we were in because we all wanted to start with anger and fear, and we had to tell those things they weren't invited to our party. I got loud. I became one of those obnoxious people who posts the same thing to Facebook every day, and I shared my blessings. I did it on days when I hurt. I did it on days when I was still battling the crippling depression that was eventually diagnosed as post-traumatic stress disorder. I made my praise loud in the best way I knew, which was social media. Some days, people jumped in and shared theirs back. One woman even started sharing her own "happy things" each day. I'm not sure of her stance on God, but she was willing to look for the joy anyway. It's a start.

Maybe Facebook isn't your thing. The important part is to find your joy and then make it loud—let people watch how God is moving in you. Planetshakers' song *Nothing is Impossible* is directly responsible for no less than 30 people staring at me at traffic lights while I danced in my car and turned up the volume. Find the joy God has for you in your situation, and don't care who sees it.

With each day, it got easier to see what Lisa called "God winks." Changing my attitude definitely helped, but I still needed more. I had been a unicorn previously, but this time I was beyond magic and sparkles; I needed help and someone to fight for me. Big Daddy Weave's *The Lion and the Lamb* had recently come out, and I self-elected to change my spirit animal to a lion. Where last time I remembered inherently that God was fighting my battles, this time I had to force that through my head. I was frequently listening to this song on Mach 20 in my ear buds reminding myself of Deuteronomy 1:30-31, "The Lord your God, who is going before you, will fight for you as He did in Egypt, before your very eyes, and in the wilderness. There you saw how the Lord your God carried you, as a father carries his son, all the way you went until you reached this place."

> *Our God is a Lion, the Lion of Judah*
> *He's roaring with power, and fighting our battles*
> *…who can stop the Lord Almighty?*

Nobody. That's who.

I reminded myself of that even when it was hard. At some point I heard an Eddie Izzard bit where he talks about giving people the option of cake or death. I'm not really sure where I heard it because his type of humor isn't really my jam. I assume a friend posted a clip to Facebook or something, but I felt like that skit summed up how I felt. When my radiation oncologist started going over the side effects of full spine radiation with me, I responded, "I know, I know, but radiation or death." I feel like that about all the options. Chemo or death, radiation or death, but ultimately, trust or death. I reminded myself that my God was a lion roaring with power and fighting my battles, so I could choose trust. I never did have someone offer me cake—all my choices seemed much harder—but I am still stubbornly clinging to the truth that I can do all things because Christ will give me strength. Even if it's not an easy choice.

And yes, I just took a religious subject and related it to Eddie Izzard. So there. Proof I can do all things.

God Winks, So Look

I am pretty sure I'm somewhere at the beginning of "the millennials." Unfortunately, my generation as a group has turned pretty hard from God in lieu of spiritualism, the universe, or just flat-out science-worship/atheism. I know a lot of them look down on my identification of good as being God, but the thing is, with people being allowed to give words power and "self-identify" in so many ways, I am unwilling and unable to give up calling the good things in my life by their actual name. I know we already covered this, but could I call all these things coincidences? Could I call them all the universe speaking to me? Sure. I could totally do that. However, I know there is something bigger than me, something in control when I feel out of control, and I know placing my trust in that something has never, ever let me down. I know the things I read in the Bible about this thing that is bigger than me are true and have not failed me. I know I have been surrounded by love in these situations, and

148

the Bible tells us God is love. Accepting that premise—that the things in my life have occurred to lift me up and show me that God is love—is my truth. That's my self-identification of what's happening in my life. That's how this is going for me. In fact, I would challenge anyone who calls the good things and inspiring coincidences in their life "the universe" or "funny" to try calling them "God" for a few weeks. It doesn't change that they happened, but it makes them mean so much more when the God that loves you is aligning them, rather than random fate just happening upon you.

Here are a few of my favorite "God winks" from my second round of ependymoma. We started calling my tumors, collectively, Slim Shady because of the rap song. I had interesting and eclectic taste in music in high school. Guess who's back again? Shady's back, so we called it that.

- In the nursing area of radiation oncology, I met a woman who had been dealing with her ependymoma for years and was still going strong. She was also a patient of my oncologist. With ependymoma's being such a rare cancer in adults, it was amazing to meet another ependymoma patient, let alone one with such a positive outlook on living with her disease.
- My first-ever niece was born on World Brain Tumor Day.
- The surgeon that spoke with Austin after my surgery said my tumor certainly looked grade III, but we'd have to wait for the formal report. We worked on that thought until returning and finding out it was only a grade II.
- Leaving the hospital after my surgery, there was a giant rainbow in the window. It was the first thing I got to sit up and see. Rainbows remind us that God keeps his promises.
- Driving home from my surgery two days later, we saw six rainbows.

- My friend Lisa kept telling me "fear is not part of the plan" and my oncologist at Duke said those exact words to me at our initial meeting.
- I received almost the same prayer vision from two separate people at two separate churches. I call them the Catholic and Protestant versions—one was Mary standing behind me with her mantle over my back and the other was Jesus standing behind me with his mantle over my back, both with the message that God very literally "had my back." My oncologist then said that she had my back, too.

A Few Thoughts on Fear

My amazing friend, Lisa, walked with me through both of my diagnoses (diagnosi? I'm not sure. I think this means you shouldn't ever have to pluralize the word diagnosis.) She kept reminding me that "fear is not part of the plan." In fact, after weeks of her telling me that, my oncologist at Duke told me the same thing—it was one of the amazing God moments that helped me know I was on the right track.

And here's the thing about fear. It's a liar. Will Smith, who is not Jesus but got this right, said in *After Earth*, "Do not misunderstand me, danger is very real, but fear is a choice." God rejects fear again and again and again. Look at Isaiah 41:13, "For I am the Lord your God who takes hold of your right hand and says to you, 'Do not fear, I will help you.'" According to Rick Warren (who has probably counted—I have not), the Bible says "Fear not" 365 times. That's one time for every day of your year, and even if it were only in there once (definitely more—I've counted that much) it would still be true. I'm pretty sure God doesn't want you to fear.

Now, if only it were that easy. God says, "Fear not;" my friend said, "Fear is not part of the plan;" and my oncologist said "I am not scared," … so I spent what I imagine adds up to a cumulative week of my life in bed in the fetal position crying out to God—in fear. Not the first time, mind you. The first time I blindly trusted Him. The second time, however, I was scared and most of that from a very specific lack of trust. I didn't trust that God was big enough to show more mercy than I could fathom. He'd spared me once from this cancer, and He'd gotten me through a sixteen-hour brain surgery unscathed. He let me get back to "normal" and raise my babies and raise money to fight brain cancer. He was so good. In my mind, this meant I must have used up all of my "points" with God. He had already given me all of the mercy and grace I could possibly be worthy of, and then some.

But God is infinitely bigger than I gave him credit for, something I am infinitely repentant of. Just because I can't fathom God thinking I am worthy of more grace or more mercy doesn't mean God thinks I'm small and unworthy. He let His son suffer and die for me, so I'm sure that means He thinks I'm worthy of just about anything.

Going back to Will Smith for a minute, he makes an excellent point. The danger in walking across a tightrope is that you'll fall. However, the fear in walking across a tightrope is in thinking you'll do just that. What if, instead of letting your mind ask, "What if I fall?" you reinforced yourself with the "fear not" message and ask yourself, "What if I fly?" What if, when faced with a terrible diagnosis you asked yourself "What if I am a survivor?" instead of asking yourself a million questions related to "What if I don't make it?" It's hard and requires constant mental power to make yourself do it. Choosing faith over fear is exhausting at times. I noticed the worse my physical pain was during treatment, the harder it was to maintain my mental balance and ability to focus on good possibilities and not negative fears.

Choosing to focus on positives as possibilities and not negatives is also difficult because as people we like to plan. As a mother, asking myself, "What if I don't make it out of this?" allowed me to come up with a plan for my children. I was able to select a school I felt comfortable with them attending since homeschool wouldn't work if I was dead. I was able to leave instructions for my funeral with a trusted pastor because my Jewish husband wasn't going to know how I wanted my Christian funeral service to look. I wrote notes and updated my will—and those aren't bad things. Doing all that helped me to look that fear in the eye and tell it "If I die, then my children will be fine." And for every fear, there is a promise that God has for you. In the case of worrying about my children, I know that Jeremiah 29:11 applies to my children just as much as to me. God has good plans for them, plans to prosper them and not to harm them. And he has those plans for me, too—even if his plan isn't for me to live.

Contrary to What Your Teacher Told You, There are Stupid Questions

I remember being in elementary school and sitting through teachers spending twenty minutes explaining how to do the worksheet (helpful hint: write the correct answer) and then asking if anyone had questions followed by, "There's no such thing as a stupid question!" Someone would then take it upon themselves to be like, "No stupid question? Shoot-—hold my juice box," and they would proceed to ask a totally asinine question like whether or not we should write our names on the paper or whether we could write in crayon instead of pencil, or my personal favorite, "Can I go to the bathroom?"

In the case where you or someone you love is ill, there are some stupid questions, and I'm just going to tell you that up front. Let's start with "Why is this happening to me?" Now, if you are both a patient and a cancer researcher or geneticist, I retract my comments, and you should figure that out. Right now. Hurry up, because there are a lot of us waiting. However, if you're asking that question in terms of "I'm such a good person, why is this happening to me?" or "Why am I sick when there are people like (insert dictator here) on the earth?", then let me save you some time and self-torment because unless you have lung cancer and smoked for 40 years, the medical answer is a combination of genes and bad luck, and the spiritual answer is that you totally deserve this.

Yeah, I said it. You deserve it.

You don't like that answer right now, and you might be thinking about flinging this book across the room. However, follow me for just a second because the Bible is super clear on this. Romans 6:23 tells us the wages of sin is death. When sin entered the world, sickness, pain, and death came, too. It's like when a girl goes to the bathroom, she's going to take a posse with her. Since we are all sinners (Romans again, 3:23), we all deserve death. The real question you should be asking yourself "why me" about is why you are in the position you are in to ask that question. What I deserve is to have been born in poverty in a war-famished third-world country where I never know health, security, or happiness, and to die alone condemned to an eternity in hell. But I was born in America where I am still here to ask why this is happening to me since I have access to medical care and treatment that some people can't even dream about. I deserved to die a slow, painful death because of my initial brain tumor. Every day I can be here and think, *"Did this BPA in the water bottles give me cancer?"* is a #FirstWorldProblems massive blessing on my life.

What I got is Jesus dying for me on the cross so I can know that I win even if I die.

When you start to reframe your reference and know you deserve death but Christ came to give you life, your whole worldview changes. When you start from a place of "I don't deserve this," but you're referring

156 | I Quit

to your blessings and not your curses, you change what you're looking for and how you feel about everything.

You know another stupid question? "Why isn't God just healing me?" Why is it stupid? Well, first of all, because you are trying to fit God into a box where He works the way you would work. If we could have it our way, nobody we love would ever get sick, or suffer, or die. But God's ways are bigger than ours, and frankly, while you can sometimes look back and see what He was doing in a situation when it's over, sometimes you're just going to have to trust that His way is bigger than your way. Why else is it a stupid question? Because He told you already.

Suffering makes us more compassionate (2 Corinthians 1:3-5). Suffering refines us into better people (Isaiah 48:10). Suffering conforms us into God's image (Romans 8:28-29). Suffering makes us mature as people (James 1:2-4). If you let it, suffering can even make you closer with God (Job 42:5). I mentioned already that I think much of "adulting" these situations is telling your inner 2-year-old you can't always get what you want. Loudly asking why you can't have that cookie, or announcing you aren't going to get that shot, or you don't want to do this is not going to make your situation any better. It's not going to make you mentally any stronger, and honestly, the nurses will probably start looking at you a little funny. You can look at your life and decide to ask these questions and make yourself crazy, or you can supply yourself with perspective, choose to not ask them, and keep going.

Keep going.

You Keep Using That Word.
I Don't Think It Means What
You Think It Means.

I've mentioned a few times before that I recoil from the word "Survivor." Early on, I didn't identify with the word survivor since I felt my diagnosis wasn't as bad as someone else's, and I felt like I hadn't suffered sufficiently to earn the title. I felt like I was somehow faking.

Now, I feel like survivor isn't the correct term to use for most brain cancer patients. The word survivor has a connotation that you're finished. I realize it's used as a noun, and not as a past tense verb, as in "I survived," but it still seems like the wrong word to describe what I'm doing. I haven't finished dealing with my ependymoma, and I may never finish dealing with my ependymoma. I could be doing this until I die or Jesus comes back. I'm living with my diagnosis, but I don't feel like I've survived it because I'm not done.

Additionally, in light of the survival rate in brain cancer right now, survivor seems like a cruel joke. Putting someone with six to eighteen months to live in a "Survivor" shirt, while it might make someone feel empowered, makes me feel like we aren't acknowledging the truth of what's happening. Even listening to the introductions at the Race for Hope show how out of place that word seems. I believe in 2017 we had almost 10,000 walkers. Of those, we had 200 "survivors," most of who were still in the middle of treatment.

Many were not at the 2018 race because treatment did not cure them.

It just seems that, much like Inego Montoya says in *The Princess Bride*, we keep saying the word survivor, and I don't think that word means what they think it means. If you feel empowered by calling yourself a survivor, even if you're still in the middle of treatment, even if your condition will be chronic, then I am so happy for you. For me, I'm still searching for a word that conveys what I am—no, I'm not dead yet, so I'm technically still "surviving," but I feel like there has to be a better way to refer to the people who are in the middle of everything, people who aren't done yet, who are still looking at the finish line in the distance. I'm not sure what word it is, but I definitely know what it's not.

Some Thoughts on the
Whole "Warrior" Thing

I completely understand that some people embrace the cancer warrior mentality. It helps them to cope and to feel empowered. I *hate* the "warrior" thing, and I especially hate it when people say that someone "lost their battle" with cancer. I wrote this after someone posted that a member of our running group had "lost her battle with cancer," rather than responding on Facebook. I ugly cried the whole time. I know my response was about me, and not about her—I didn't know her—but I share it here in case that verbiage hurts you in the same way it hurts me.

Someone Important Died Today
Someone important died today.
While I was obsessing over dropping my child off at a program taking him away from me for six weeks, while I was watching my

middle son's hockey game, while I was busy with my life, someone important slipped out of this life and into the next.

I didn't know her, this important person, but she was one of those people I feel like I should have known. The art teacher of a friend's children, a member of a running club I was in, Facebook friend of so many of my Facebook friends—in a game of Kevin Bacon, she and I are only one degree apart.

And, when I found out that she died, I was angry. Angry that my child will, hopefully, get more time with me and her sweet babies will not get more with her. Angry that someone so young and vibrant was taken from the rest of us. And angry at the people talking about how she "lost her fight."

I know that over the years the "warrior" mentality has become pervasive among those surrounding people facing cancer. "Fight Like a Girl!" exclaims every pink yogurt carton, handkerchief, and shirt on the market. "Warrior," writes Ford Motor Company over the black and white image of a defiant-looking bald woman with her hands on her hips. "Just keep fighting," exclaims every visitor you see on a bad day when the chemo or the radiation or the nausea is just a tiny bit more than you can take right now.

I know they say it because they don't know.

They don't know that a fight with cancer isn't like a thumb war or a fistfight or even a fight with your best friend where you both play dirty with passive-aggressive Facebook rants. It's not a fight with your sister with hair pulling and favorite sweater burning. It's not a fight for that last rep in weight lifting or that last mile of a race. It's not even an MMA cage fight. All of those fights, ultimately, have someone watching—someone that will tell you it's over, someone that will establish rules—but cancer doesn't do rules. Cancer cheats.

Cancer comes for you before you even realize you're fighting. It comes when you're on top of your game—when you're running 40 miles a week and drinking smoothies. It comes to set you up so you're already off-balance when it takes its first real swing at you.

It comes first for your sanity.

You're tired, you're getting more bruises, you're getting headaches, you can't tolerate foods that you used to. You lost weight, you gained weight, something feels tender or swollen. When you finally stop making excuses and go to the doctor, they tell you that it's not a big deal. In my case, I had headaches for months and finally went to the doctor only to be told that I was having migraines and they were "normal" and that I needed to learn to "deal with them." They told me I was weak. That it was nothing. That I was crazy.

And then, cancer comes for your family.

When you finally get that phone call telling you that there's actually something wrong (or that office visit, nurse email, whatever you received), then cancer comes for your family. I don't think that it takes anyone with children more than ten seconds to go from "Oh sweet God I don't want to die" to "What am I going to tell my children?" Cancer makes you see fear in your children's eyes where once there was only joy. It makes your spouse hold you like an object that might break instead of like an object of affection.

Then comes that first punch. It comes for your body.

The surgery, the chemo, the drugs, the pain, the radiation, the endless IVs that blow your veins, the side effects——they start now that your corner is off balance. It hurts and you're tired and some days you may even wish it would all just end. But while you're down from that, cancer doesn't quit——it comes with a cheap kick while you're down.

Cancer comes for your identity.

It takes your hair, takes your skin tone, takes your titles. "The red-head lady who runs the PTA" turns into the bald, slightly green woman who doesn't do anything but vomit. Gone are your looks, gone are the responsibilities that defined you, gone are your hobbies. But, as you continue—shell of who you were, to continue dealing with the repeated physical abuse—cancer brings in help.

Cancer comes for your friendships.

They don't mean to—I know they don't—but cancer somehow manages to recruit your friends to deliver cheap shots. Relatives, too. Especially the ones with "in-law" after their name. "You're getting stronger every day." POW! "God wouldn't give you this if he didn't think you could handle it." SMACK! They've got a platitude for everything, and they all sting—rubbing salt in the wounds you already had. "Your kids are going to learn to be so strong and independent with you not around to do anything for them!" Gut punch.

And, of course, cancer can try for other things, too. Your faith, your career, your financial stability—nothing is out of its scope or desire to steal.

And then when someone succumbs to the illness, coming at them from every angle people say, "She was such a fighter, but the cancer beat her." "She tried so hard, but she just couldn't fight hard enough."

What a shallow understanding you have.

There is no winning or losing here. You don't "win" because you managed to battle your way through the treatments and entered remission—you don't magically feel like yourself again, you don't instantly survive. You spend years fighting your way back to a new "normal" that you can live with, and you hold your breath every few months until the requisite number of years pass before they can officially say you are cancer-free. Even after that, you panic every time you show the mildest symptom that could be explained by the return of the beast that tried to kill you before. And you don't lose because you took your cancer to the ground. You didn't give up or abandon the good fight because your body couldn't take anymore.

A beautiful, vibrant, special, adored woman died today. She exiled the rogue cells that were eating her alive to the ground where they will rot and die. They can't hurt her anymore. They can't grow any further. She will continue to shine. Whether you believe in heaven—I do—and think that her soul lives on in paradise, or you believe in just the here and now where people remember every good thing she did and are coming together in her memory and her children live on in her image, she keeps going.

In both scenarios—live or die—there is pain. There is pain of loss whether from ability or physical stamina, or loss due to death. There is joy, whether from survival or from memories. This isn't a game of tic-tac-toe where there is one clear winner and one clear loser. Cancer is a game of monopoly where four days of playing later, exhausted, frustrated, and broke, no one is really a winner— someone just has more cards.

Someone died today. She took her cancer to the ground where it can't hurt her anymore. She isn't a failed warrior—she is someone who overcame, even if it's not in the way you would have preferred. Honor her by not making her out to be the loser in a clear-cut fight. Honor her by remembering every amazing thing she did and how brightly her star continues to shine for those who love her.

Lord, Please Keep Making Me

I feel like I need to tell you about the people this has made us into. There's a cliché story out there about a chef who puts an egg, some coffee, and a potato in boiling water. The story goes that each of these things were put into the same situation. The egg went in soft inside, but the water turned it hard throughout. The potato went in hard, but the water made it into a mashable mess. The coffee, however, went in and changed the water. Now, am I saying my experiences changed the cancer game? Absolutely not. I did not find a cure or a new treatment, or really a new way of doing things, but I like to think I took the water I was placed into and dealt with it on my terms, even when I had to try hard to ensure we were using my rules, and not the water's.

I think my experiences have made me a better version of who I already was. I obviously didn't give up my humor, in fact, my ability to find the funny in everything is part of what has helped me to cope. However, my compassion was sharpened on such a high level I don't even believe I knew what that word meant before. That first shower I took was glorious, but it also hurt the side of my body with the neuropathy, and I suddenly understood why my grandmother, a stroke victim, used to scream no matter what temperature we made the water. When I see someone with a feeding tube and a bald head, there is a respect I grant to them as fellows, rather than strangers. I know that anyone could be suffering underneath their exterior, and I try to be sensitive to that, although it remains difficult with people who work at insurance call centers.

I feel like I look at myself with a lot more grace than I ever gave myself before. I might be fluffy, but I am strong. I might have wrinkles under my eyes due to my very thin and very dry chemo skin, but they're from smiling. There's an adage that age is a privilege denied to many, but luckily, if that privilege is denied to me, I am getting a jump start on it with Mylanta in my purse, a pill box in my pocket (which I covered in glitter), and getting shingles at the ripe old age of thirty-three. Understanding how waking up every day in pain, how your body betraying you can feel, these things have made me more tolerant of both those around me who are aging, and with myself as I try to marvel at what I can do instead of hating myself for what I can't.

I am confident I have learned I can, in fact, 1 Corinthians 10:31—I like the King James here—says, "whatsoever ye do, do all to the glory of God." I can have cancer to the glory of God. I can take chemo to the glory of God. I can post to Facebook to the glory of God. That doesn't mean that I've nailed it completely, but in all circumstances, if I use what I know about God and who He says He is, and that I can trust him when I act like the person He tells me in the Bible I am, I can do everything for his glory.

Conversely, I've learned that Philippians 4:13 is an encouragement, not a challenge. "I can do all things through Christ who strengthens me' does not mean I have to do all the things. There are no medals for doing

166 | I Quit.

this by yourself. There is no award given out for continuing to put on makeup and working twelve hours and doing it all while being treated for chemo. There is no punishment for admitting that you need help. Sometimes, that "through Christ" part is literal—you can do anything when you trust Christ to give you the internal strength to face fear, disease, and even death. Sometimes, though, that "through Christ" part is a reference to his body here on earth, the people who are surrounding you wanting to be his hands and feet. Don't deny him the right to help you in either instance.

I value my husband and my children more than I ever did when I failed to realize how finite and precious they are. My marriage is stronger—I joke that my husband loves me more than Edward loved Bella—but I'm only half joking. He would do anything for me, and in return, it is my pleasure to show him reciprocal love, even if it's only me trying to keep the house clean because I know that's his favorite thing.

While this was awful in many ways, and while the pain and the heartache, and even the depression was all very real, the benefits are very real, too. I am more patient, more faithful, more compassionate, a better mother, a better wife, a more understanding friend, all because I have walked through this fire, and honestly, because it's burned me—and I like to think that what it burned off needed to go anyway.

I'm also constantly amazed at who this has made my children. What kid asks, "What are you up to today, mom?" or says, "I don't want to go to the park if you can't sit in the sun with me." They understand I have limitations at times, and they don't complain about them. They understand fear in a way they shouldn't have to, but they also understand faith in a bigger way than I think I ever will. Logan prayed this prayer during my first recovery: "Dear God, thank you so much for my lunch, and for my mommy making it, even though she's sick. Please heal her and make her feel better because I love her. You are a very big God. Amen."

Wow.

Now, don't get me wrong. I know that's not taking over the place of some of the verses the psalmist penned, but what a prayer, right? So simple, and so much all at the same time. Hey God, I love this person so much, I recognize her sacrifice, and even though I see her with staples in her head and unable to do everything, I know you can fix her."

Riley is an outspoken advocate for things like health care reform, which is hilarious because he's fourteen, but he knows how much it's meant to our family that I can get the medication and surgeries that I need. He's also aware of when the system fails. One of our local politicians lost his wife to cancer, and Riley wrote him a letter because he'd worked with him during the page program and wanted him to know he could understand how hard cancer could be. Logan is compassionate and can identify other children who need someone to wrap an arm around them and love them, even without words. Savannah would be a warrior princess if she didn't hate the second word, so I'll just call her a prayer warrior. When we pray as a family at night, she remembers faithfully to pray for friends of our family with cancer, especially other children. She has zero hesitation when asked if God is in control of their situations because she knows we are trusting God to be in control of mine. They are amazing, and I am so proud of them for being able to handle such a big, scary thing with so much grace, and to come out of the other side refined and better—just like I'm trying to.

So, We Need to Wrap This Up.

I would never have asked for this, but going through it, I wouldn't take it back, either. Taking a very clear look at your life can be a great way to realize you don't regret things (like staying home with your kids) that you have questioned in the past. I see now so many little and big things that made us uniquely prepared for this situation that show me how God prepared us for it—from having our children at a young age to choosing to raise our family in an area that gave us access to incredible doctors to my physical therapist baby brother having a certification in working with patients undergoing radiation and chemotherapy, my life is covered in fingerprints of a bigger plan at work. Sometimes I've felt like I don't matter, and being surrounded by people willing to go out of their way to help my family makes me feel like a piece of a greater community.

I learned for a fact how much my husband loves me. Without one complaint or gripe or call for recognition, the man has coordinated my care, interviewed my doctors, and advocated for me when I was too weak or too drugged to do it.

So, I feel like there should be a point here. If I had to sum up, I would say:

1. Listen to your body, and don't be afraid to question a diagnosis that seems dismissive or wrong.
2. You matter to so many more people than you know.
3. Even in a really horrible situation, there are so many ways to see how blessed you are.

On my "survive-a-versary" in 2017, knowing that something was wrong, I posted this:

"There are so many reasons I am thankful for God's grace that I can be here today. Getting to see my babies grow up, watching Julian Edelman make that catch, being around to help people, time with friends, watching the leaves in the fall… Thank you to everyone who prayed for me so fervently on this day in 2013. If you need a reminder that God is gracious and answers yes sometimes, here it is."

I hope my story has been a reminder to you about the same thing. If you're going through a similar diagnosis, keep going—sometimes the answer is yes, and even if it isn't, there can be joy in each day you spend choosing it.

About the Author

Kristina Schnack Kotlus doesn't like writing about herself in the third person, so biographies are hard for her. She feels like you really should have picked up on who she is by reading this book, but if you didn't, she'll recap:

Kristina Schnack Kotlus is a two-time brain cancer "survivor" (although she hates that word). She was baptized a Lutheran, tried atheism because of the Anglicans, worked for the Methodists, and now attends an Assemblies of God congregation. She has a degree in Comparative Religion from the secular George Mason University by way of Jesuit Holy Cross College, and she's married to a non-practicing Jew. She's trying hard to win ecumenicalism. She's written for her own website, PwcMoms, for years, helping parents in Prince William County, Virginia, feel more connected to where they live. She's been published in numerous local magazines and newspapers, and was recognized as Blogger of the Year in Northern Virginia, 40 Under 40 in Northern

Virginia, and an Influential Woman in Prince William County. She resides in Manassas, Virginia, with her husband and three children, who she educates at home.

www.KristinaKotlus.com

Facebook.com/KristinaKotlus

Instagram: KristinaKotlus

Twitter @KristinaKotlus

CPSIA information can be obtained
at www.ICGtesting.com
Printed in the USA
JSHW022132220620
6318JS00002B/2

9 781642 795318